D1125859

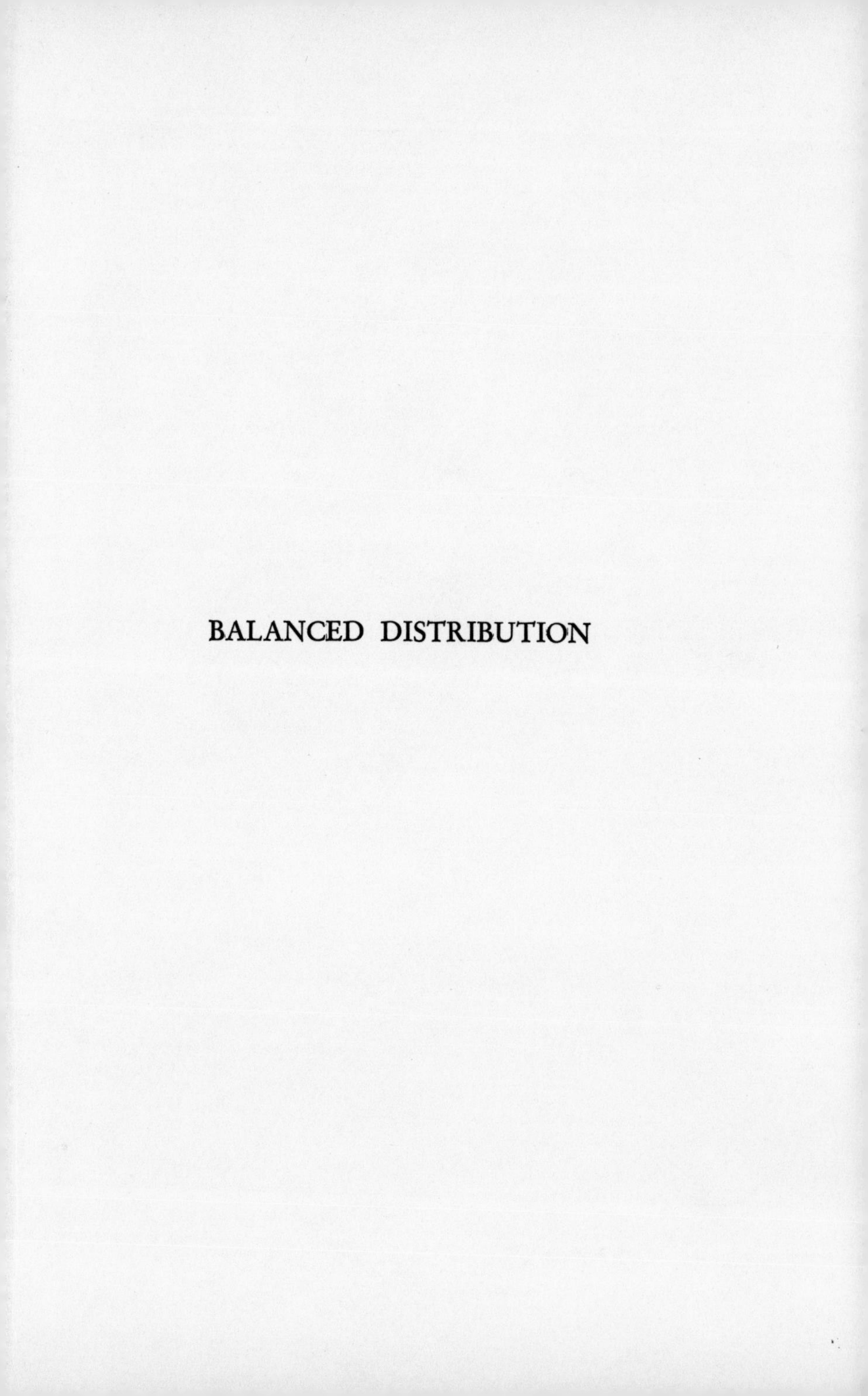

BALANCED DISTRIBUTION

BALANCED DISTRIBUTION

by

GUSTAV ERICKSON

PHILOSOPHICAL LIBRARY
New York

Philosophical Library, Inc.

15 East 40th Street, New York 16, N.Y.

Library of Congress Catalog Card Number: 64-13322

Printed in the United States of America

CONTENTS

CHAPTER I

THE COMMUNIST CHALLENGE

CHAPTER II

THE PROBLEM OF DISTRIBUTION

CHAPTER III

PURCHASING POWER

CHAPTER IV

PRICES AND SALES RESISTANCE

CHAPTER V

PRICE CONTROL

CHAPTER VI

PRICE CONTROL METHODS

CHAPTER VII

CREDIT AND CREDIT CONTROL

CHAPTER VIII

CONTROL OF DISTRIBUTION

CHAPTER IX

CONFLICTING SOCIAL OBJECTIVES

PREFACE

At no time in our economic history has there been a more urgent need than at present for a plan to deal with the problem of distribution, not to say that our Western economy has deteriorated in recent years, not that it has been brought to a point at which it no longer satisfies our immediate economic needs, not even that it shows signs of deteriorating and becoming impractical in the near future, but because it lacks the impetus, the prosperity, and the growth potential that it needs to meet the challenge of today's conflicting international ideologies. The communist threat to our free democracy is real, and to ignore it would be hazardous. If it were not for this threat, if we had nothing whatsoever to fear from the economic warfare now being waged by the communist countries, we could undoubtedly carry on for many more years without a major change, despite glutted markets, idle machinery, and unemployment. We could, perhaps, improve on our welfare program, distribute more unemployment benefits, more relief, more social assistance. We could also, perhaps, relieve our glutted markets by the desperate act of dumping and destroying goods. The time has come, however, when a defective system is no longer good enough. If we are to safeguard our cherished system of free enterprise, we must learn how to distribute and come into possession of the goods we can produce.

There is, to be true, no lack of plans, suggestions, campaigns, and activities aimed at solving the problem of distribution. The fact is that this problem, which includes a chronic shortage of purchasing power, a market overstocked with unsold goods and services, plants and machinery standing idle, and men out of work, has been subject to more censuring criticism, more rebuke, and more attempted amelioration than any other problem. Economists, government advisors, and public representatives have handed out millions of words of advice on how to cope with the problem; political parties have pressured for reforms intended to bring prosperity and full employment; one government after another has taken office with the earnest intention to do away with unemployment; but the problem still persists as it has done for generations; and there is a strong suspicion on the part of some people that private enterprise must be sacrificed before the problem can be solved, or that any plan which will effectively deal with the problem will involve the establishment of socialism or communism.

It is true, indeed, that strong government action will be necessary before the problem can be conquered. This problem of distribution will not resolve itself. If we confine our actions to the exigency of handing out relief to those who are thrown out of employment or to the compassionate act of easing pain suffered by the victims but do nothing toward removing the cause of the trouble, the problem will in all certainty continue as before. But the necessary or proper action in this case is not the establishment of socialism, either the one form or the other, but the control of purchasing power. The ownership of the instruments of production has nothing in itself to do with the problem of distribution or its solution. Overstocked market inventories and unemployment are caused by an insufficiency of purchasing power, and the right action to take is that which will supplement this deficiency. We do not aspire to government controls which do not advance our cause. In a free democracy we want the maximum of freedom and the minimum of social control, yet the measure of control which will ensure a balanced distribution; and the only way to realize this ideal is to take the right action, no more and no less.

This book might have been entitled *How to Create Purchasing Power* or *How to Control and Balance Purchasing Power to Ensure Full Capacity Production.* But whatever the title, its aim is to contribute its share to the store of knowledge and information that must be mastered in the near future if we are to conquer this greatest-of-all problems in our economic history, the problem of distribution. The subject matter has been confined mainly to generalities, or macroeconomics, to save space and to emphasize the general principle and purpose of distribution control. It seeks to answer such questions as: What is the problem of distribution? How serious is this problem, economically, socially, politically (chapters I and II)? What is the cause of the problem? How could the problem be intensified, relieved, or reversed (chapter III)? What kind of reform is necessary, and how will this reform affect our free-enterprise economy? What public reaction is likely to result (chapter V)? How will the reform be put into force? What fundamental changes in theory, economic thought, and national ambitions are likely to ensue? Efforts have been made to render the material easily comprehensible to the average reader, or the layman.

G. Erickson
Richmond, B.C.

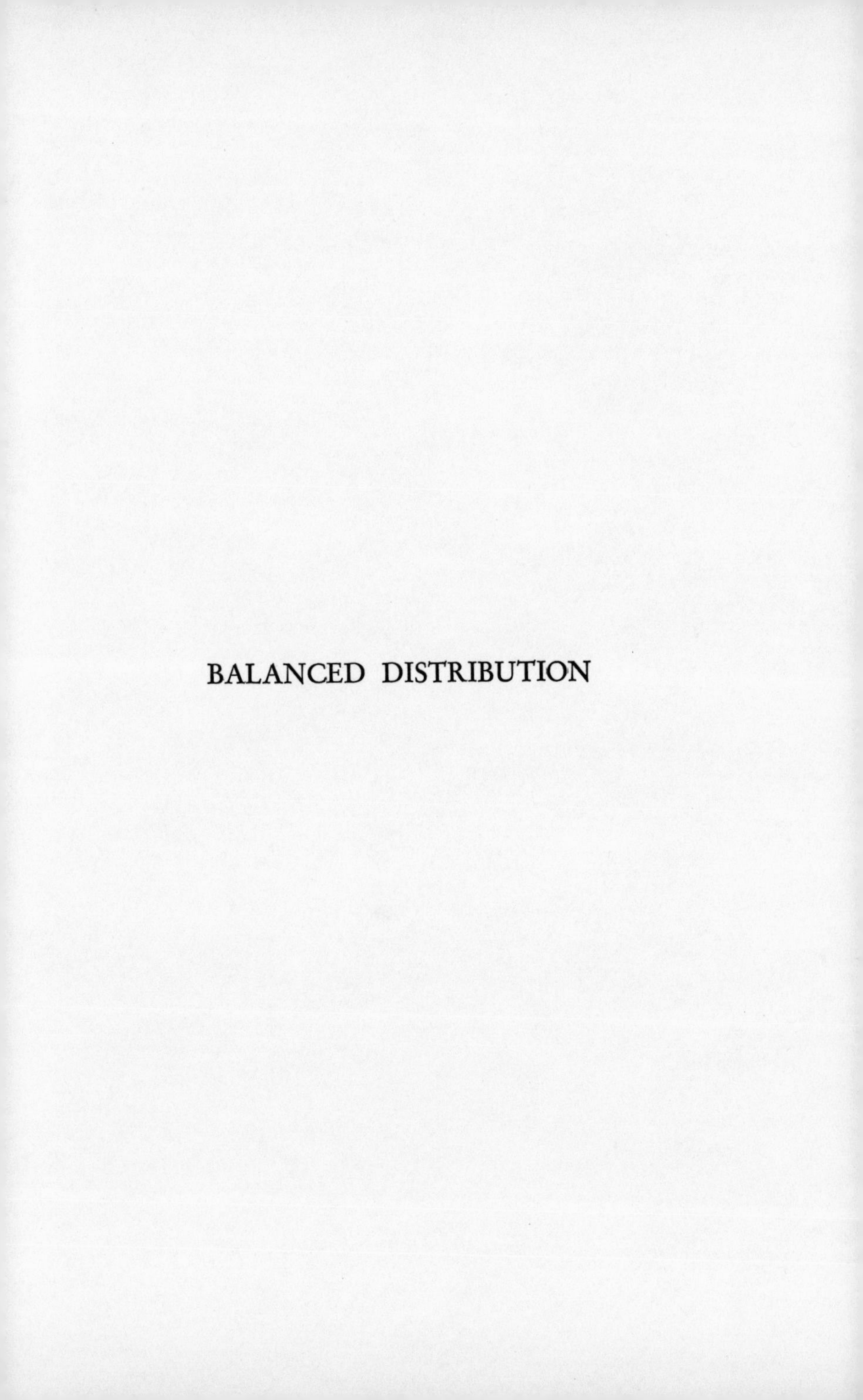

BALANCED DISTRIBUTION

CHAPTER I

THE COMMUNIST CHALLENGE

"Your grandchildren will live under communism"

Nikita Khrushchev—
speaking to the American people on
his visit to the United States in 1959.

1. The Possibilities of a Communist Victory

It is commonly held in the Soviet Union and in other countries of the communist world that the capitalist system is doomed, that it "carries the seed of its own destruction" and must ultimately collapse and be replaced by communism. And the basis of this reasoning, as we know, is that the communist countries will emerge victors in the prevailing struggle to build a greater and more abundant social and economic life; that they will overtake the West in physical volume of production, social well-being, and national prestige; and that therefore, true to the theory *the survival of the fittest,* the capitalist system must inevitably succumb.

What chance is there that this communist prediction will hold true, assuming, of course, that no nuclear war will disrupt the course of progress, and also that no significant change in our economic setup is forthcoming? Will communists under these circumstances succeed in establishing a more popularly acceptable social order than our own, thus jeopardizing free democracy?

Most of us, undoubtedly, would answer this question in the negative. We might assume, on the other hand, that the very opposite is true, that people in communist countries will eventually demand the freedom of ownership and enterprise enjoyed in the West, and that communism on this account will recede. None of us, however, could escape the feeling that a threat exists, or that the communist prophecy possesses some evidence of logic. In fact, there is a great deal of concern over the material success of communism, not least among Americans, whose stake in free enterprise is the greatest. There are certain definite circumstances favoring communism, circumstances which indicate that a communist victory might be considered possible. The first and most important of these is, of course, our own inability to speed up, or to bring into the economic race the idle men and idle machinery which now lie dormant and wasted because of the lack of markets. Our rate of economic growth is generally limited to the rate at which goods are purchased or taken off the market; but there seems to be nothing that we can do, politically or otherwise, to accelerate this process. As a rule we must depend on forces beyond our control to bring prosperity. We could, perhaps, purchase large quantities of goods with public money and give these goods away to some other country, stock them up, or destroy them; but such a program would not win a race with communism. It would involve taxing the public in order to reduce the wealth at our disposal. Nor could we give these goods to our own people, since this would reduce demand and create more marketing difficulties. As an alternative, we might consider purchasing the goods with new money added to the circulation, but this would simply cause price inflation and further weakening of the economy. We might also, perhaps, create work by placing men in non-productive occupations, making sure that they did not produce goods to flood the market. But again, this would not add to the nation's wealth in a bid to outdo communism. It is safe to say that under present conditions we are poorly equipped to meet communism on the economic battlefield.

A second circumstance favorable to a communist victory is the relentless determination by communists, especially in the Soviet Union, to win the economic battle. They are fully aware of our difficulties, and they will spare no effort to take advantage of them. Being conscious of the economic growth rate of each country, especially that of America as compared with their own, they are determined to keep a step ahead, to advance a little more and a little faster than ourselves, and to remain on the winning side until victory. To them the economic battle is a life-and-death struggle.

They are convinced that winning the economic battle means winning the world for communism, and to this end they have committed themselves. Their aim is to produce more steel, more food, more housing; to build more factories, power dams, and industrial plants; to erect public buildings, hospitals, and schools; to build cities, streets and highways; to provide more and better communication facilities, better health services, more social security; to create a richer economic and social life, a utopia of abundance; to raise the physical and educational standards of the population; to turn out engineers, scientists, and technicians; to excel in scientific achievements, in physical discoveries, in space exploration — in short, to do anything and everything that will capture the fancy of men to the cause of communism, and to prove to the world that communism is the better bet. Their object is victory on the economic front, and they will strain every nerve to reach this objective. Each gain in their economy as compared with our own means another milestone; and the nearer they come to the final triumph of overtaking us, the more energetic they will carry on to victory. They are convinced that when communism leads the world in material well-being, people will rally to the cause of communism; and it will be only a matter of time until our "decadent" system will capitulate and when "we will bury you."

A third circumstance which also favors communism is that an economic campaign such as that described above has the advantage of being immune to outside interference. Contrary to a military campaign, it is a legitimate warfare, a warfare which cannot justly be stopped or hampered by any political opponent. We have no moral or ethical right to interfere with the economic progress in another country, even if this progress should be designed to outdo or undermine our own economy. Nor can we refute the dictum that "of their fruit ye shall know them." There is nothing sinister in a program of building factories and steel mills and homes. Each nation must have the full right to put its own house in order, and to feel resentment against such a progress would be to admit a condition of weakness. If we believe in our own system of free enterprise, we must stand by it, and we must remove any obstacle which might hinder this system from operating to full advantage. We must establish a system that is better, more progressive, more dynamic, and more socially acceptable than communism. There is no other fair way to stop communism, and there is no other road to victory.

2. The Wrong Defense Policy

What do we do today, in America for example, to meet this communist challenge? This question is crucial, for upon it depends our future welfare. The answer is that we do little of any consequence on the economic front. We leave our economic problems more or less to take care of themselves, hoping for the best. In the meantime we build an arsenal of military strength in preparation for a showdown battle with communism. We build a ring of steel around the Soviet Union. We station troops in all parts of the world where there is a possibility of communist expansion. We train millions of men for combat readiness. We invent more lethal weapons, more destructive bombs, more accurately guided missiles.

What does this all mean? Does it mean that we have abandoned hope of competing on the economic front? Does it mean that we have accepted defeat economically and must now depend on military means for our survival? Does it mean that we are prepared to wait until communism has passed us by on the economic and social fields and threaten the disintegration of our free democracy? And then will we drop the bomb and perhaps put an end to human life and all that we have struggled for in years and centuries gone by?

Whatever the answer may be, one thing can be said for certain, that this dependence on military defense alone is a dangerous and foolish game. Even admitting that military preparedness is necessary to deter aggression, we must not forget that military warfare in this atomic age cannot bring victory, nor can it preserve free democracy. It is on the economic front that the decisive battle between communism and free enterprise must be fought, and whether we can succeed in perpetuating free enterprise will depend on our success or failure in solving the problem of distribution and in establishing a more abundant and more agreeable economic life. An economic war may not produce heroes, but it is more equitable, more potent, and more decisive than a military conflict. It is constructive, not destructive. It is a warfare that can bring true victory, not devastation and ruin.

Military action to stop communism is not only treacherous and foolish, it is needless. We have all the necessary means at our disposal to fight a winning battle against communism on the economic front. We have the manpower, the resources, the incentives, and the know-how. Our producers and manufacturers are ready to produce in abundance anything that we may dream of or have use of with far greater zeal and enthusiasm than is possible under communism. We have machinery and millions of men standing idle, ready at a moment's notice to join in the battle for abundance, and to pursue the economic campaign to a successful conclusion. What we must do is to accept the economic challenge of communism, to turn our attention away from the military front and the cold war and concentrate our efforts on the economic front. Some day, perhaps, we will extend a hand of thanks to our communist competitors for this opportunity.

There is the frightening thought, however, that if we do not act promptly and with wisdom, we may perish in front of our opportunities. If the time should come when we must defend democracy by military means, our undoing may be in sight; and we could not blame anyone but ourselves, our own ignorance, our apathy, our lack of a plan to deal with the problem of distribution. We have at our disposal all the physical means to defeat communism, and to do this not at a cost to ourselves in property, monetary values, or lives, but at a tremendous gain in physical well-being. But what we must do is to orient the means by which to distribute the goods we can produce.

3. Limited Merits of Communism

At this time let us ask another crucial question: Is it possible to solve the problem of distribution within the framework of our free enterprise economy? If we should direct this question to some of our communist competitors, we would undoubtedly receive a negative answer. Balanced distribution of goods, they would say, is incompatible with private enterprise. Greedy capitalists will hold on to goods out of reach of the consuming public, and machinery and men will stand idle. The only way to solve the problem of distribution, they would suggest, is to place the instruments of production and distribution in the hands of the government, such as has been done in Russia and other communist countries.

This suggestion we cannot accept. We cannot subscribe to the doctrine that we must adopt communism as the only solution to the distributive problem. We cannot agree that we must establish precisely the system that now exists in Russia or in China; that all our farms must be collectivized or communized; that all our factories and workshops must belong to the state; or, for that matter, that all political parties must be disbanded — except one. We are ready to admit that a reform is in order, but we are not ready to sell our freedom to the dictatorial powers of a communist government. We believe there is a solution to the problem much more agreeable and much more consistent with our way of life than the establishment of a totalitarian state.

The communist argument that the solution to our problem lies in the abolition of free enterprise is based either on pure misunderstanding of the issues at hand or on a desire to justify or cover up faults in the communist system itself. The fallacy is obvious: it ignores the very nature of the problem. It presupposes that in order to solve the problem of distribution, we must take steps to reorganize production by placing farms and factories under government ownership. Nothing could be farther from the truth. Our problem is not caused by any difficulty of producing goods, but rather by the necessity of pushing these goods through the narrow bottleneck of the present market. But the proper way to solve this problem is not to break down the present productive system, but to reorganize distribution. Why should we pull the healthy tooth and leave the diseased one? If our distributive system is at fault, it seems logical that we should concentrate our initial efforts of reorganization on this sector of the economy.

The material success which is evidenced in Russia, China and elsewhere under communist rule can be attributed to either or both of two favorable circumstances applicable to communism, central planning and the absence of a distributive problem. The first of these, central planning, is particularly favorable in underdeveloped countries, countries whose industry is lagging because of the lack of capital. Private initiative is slow in developing a country because of the difficulty in obtaining the initial equipment and resources. A strong central government, such as is the principal feature of communism, is in a far better position to speed this development. By taking full ownership and control of the national resources, human as well as material, it can orient the nation's energy to the one goal of developing industry.

The second circumstance which also is very fortunate under communism is that industry and production in general are unhampered by any problem of distribution. In the Soviet Union, for instance, prices and wages are under strict government control, and anything that is produced can find a ready market. Thus, by taking control of the instruments of production and distribution, communists (in the Soviet Union) have been able, not only to develop industry at a faster rate than would have been possible under private enterprise, but have also solved the problem of distribution. These two fortunate circumstances are accountable for the material success of communism.

In America, however, and in any other highly industrialized country, we do not need communism. We do not need, for instance, a strong central government to develop industry. Our productive system is already second to none in the world. Despite the difficulties under which it labors, it is more advanced, more mechanized, and more efficient than any communist counterpart. Personal incentives are incomparably stronger and more effective than any government-imposed directives; and if the problem of distribution was solved, our economy would in all certainty leave communism hopelessly behind.

Nor do we need communism to solve the problem of distribution. This problem has to do with the relationship between prices and money incomes, not with the ownership of the instruments of production. Communism has nothing to offer in the way of guidance toward a correct distribution. Distribution in communist countries is usually as overbalanced as our own is underbalanced. The correct balancing of distribution is a project which requires strict and immaculate control, whether we have communism or not; and even admitting that the task would be simpler under full government ownership, it is definitely not a program beyond our power to consummate.

4. The Preservation of Free Enterprise

What we must recognize, however, is that an economic race exists between communism and free enterprise, and that we are in it, whether we like it or not. We may have been dragged into the race against our will; we may find it an unpleasant responsibility to pursue; we may desire to shake the yoke off our shoulders; but we cannot ignore it, for to do so would be fatal. We must run the race to the finish line, and we must win; for the winning of this race means the winning of the world.

We must recognize, also, that in this contest absolute honesty must prevail. We cannot win a just victory by acts of hostility, fear or hatred, nor even by threats of armed force. We believe in democracy and free elections; we must also leave it free for the people of the world to choose freely between the two social systems. Victory over communism lies in the establishment of a system that is better and more acceptable than communism, a system which people of their own free will will elect to follow and live under, a system free from the flaws of unemployment and poverty which now prevent the full acceptance of free enterprise and which, in fact, have created communism in the first place.

What we must remember above all is that the success and perpetuation of free enterprise does not consist in the retention of things such as they are. On the contrary, free enterprise can be retained only through the implementation of a basic reform. Nothing could be more hazardous to our cause, and nothing could give greater comfort and encouragement to our communist competitors than a determination by the West to retain the status quo.

The greatest threat to their plans of economic supremacy is the eventuality that we might release the huge productive potential that now is tied from our reach by the market bottleneck, the bottleneck upon which rests the success of communism. Their calculation of success, their estimates of economic growth of some seven or eight per cent per year as against our three or four per cent, their timetable of events in overtaking the West—all are based on the assumption that we retain the present lag in production, the present underutilization of productive capacity, and the present unemployment. The solution of the problem of distribution in the Western world would end once for all any communist hopes of winning the economic battle. Such a move, in fact, might deal a fatal blow to communism itself. It is natural, therefore, that communists should be extremely anxious to keep capitalism unchanged; and if they should feel inclined to take a helping hand in this task, the best that they could do would be to advocate in the West a laissez-faire or leave-things-alone policy, which would inhibit on our side any change in the existing order of things.

Those who today are the most anxious to retain free enterprise are likely to give the greatest encouragement to communists by their refusal to accept reforms. They believe that any plan of economic or social reform will inevitably lead to socialism or communism, and that by rejecting such reforms they are helping to preserve free enterprise. Hence they are promoting precisely the condition which communists would consider most welcome and most certain to bring a communist victory. The reason for this irony is that there is no commonly recognized plan of reform which will guarantee to solve our economic problems and yet retain free enterprise. According to communists, at least, capitalism cannot reform. It has advanced to a point at which no further advancement or improvement is possible, and the next step in the social development is communism. According to this reasoning the problem of distribution, which includes overstocked inventories, idle plants and machinery, unemployment, poverty and relief rolls, cannot be removed without removing capitalism. It implies, as our communist competitors would have us believe, that we have the choice of holding on to the last twig of capitalism for a limited period at the cost of unemployment and relief rolls, or submit to communism.

To anyone who can reason, this doctrine of despair must appear absurd. There is no logical reason to fear that a reform to solve the problem of distribution will lead to communism. This problem is caused by the flaw of underdistribution, which can quite easily be solved without sacrificing free enterprise. To abolish private enterprise, individual incentive, and personal reward for unit of output is not necessary to the balancing of distribution, and would in all certainty be a step backwards. Even the Soviet Government recognizes the necessity of personal incentives, a fact which can be verified by its efforts to introduce piecework in place of wages throughout industry. The policy which is most likely to lead to communism is the policy of inaction. What we must recognize is that a reform is necessary, a reform adequate to deal with the problem of distribution, for upon this reform rests the fate of free enterprise, and perhaps the world.

What we need above all in this emergency is the faculty of clear thinking. We cannot meet the challenge of communism by irrational impulses or emotional antagonism either on the right side or the left side of the political fence. We must use the power of logical reason and unbiased scientific thought. We must ask ourselves plainly the question: What is the nature and what is the cause of the flaw which keeps a considerable percentage of our human and material resources unutilized and wasted, and what must we do to effect a permanent cure? In the following chapter we shall endeavor to answer the first two of these questions, and shall proceed in subsequent chapters to answer the third.

CHAPTER II

THE PROBLEM OF DISTRIBUTION

The paradox of poverty amid plenty is as baffling today as it was decades ago. Throughout the years, with the exception of wartime, men have been asking the question: "Why do we suffer want of goods and services in a world in which wealth-producing machinery is standing idle and millions are denied the opportunity to work and produce?" This situation in our modern day is an affront to our intellect and our resourcefulness. Why is it that even in a space-age such as the present, when science has accomplished feats beyond our imagination, our economy should remain at a stone-age stage of development? Why do we pay farmers for not farming and workers for not working? Why do we store an ever-increasing volume of goods in government warehouses, permanently out of reach of the consumer, while a large percentage of our population cannot afford to buy the necessities for a decent standard of living? Why do we have a problem of distribution, and how has this problem arisen?

It would be vain to attempt to answer these questions in a few words or sentences, or even in a chapter; but there is one side of the question which could be answered in one single word—specialization. Specialization, the practice of specializing each in his own line of production, is, we might say, the direct cause of our present troubles. And to prove our point we might say that if people did not specialize, that is, if they should produce individually their own necessities of life in their own homes or in their own surroundings, there could never be such a thing as a problem of distribution, for the simple reason that the goods produced in this manner would already be in the hands of the person or persons who are to consume them, and there would be nothing to distribute. Our troubles are caused by the fact that under the present method of production we are producing goods which have little or no direct value to us, goods which must be disposed of in exchange for other goods produced by others. We must have our individual economic contribution recognized and accepted by the general market and, in return, be given access to the multitude of other goods and services supplied by this market; and it is the difficulty connected with this exchange that is our problem.

1. Direct Acquisition

But in order to illustrate this situation let us turn back the pages of our economic history to a time, a century or two ago, when most of the necessities of life were produced in the home by the members of the family themselves. The typical family or household at that time had within its reach the essential natural resources. It had a water supply ample for all its needs. It had cultivated land on which it produced the necessary crops of fruit, vegetables, grain, and hay. It had forests and lakes from which it received game and fish. It had timber and minerals from which it obtained materials for all necessary buildings, furnitures, and implements.

The home assumed the appearance of a small but diversified industrial state. A variety of outbuildings, each of its own utility, covered the estate, some to house cattle, horses, sheep, swine, poultry, and other animals; some to be used as storage for implements, feed, grain, and food-stuffs; some to serve as workshop, bakery, tannery, etc. Primitive implements were used to work the soil, transport materials, harvest the crops, grind the grain into flour, make furniture, and erect buildings. Domestic animals provided the family with milk, butter, cheese, eggs, meat, wool, leather and many other essentials. The housewife was milking, churning, baking, carding, spinning, weaving, knitting, and sewing. Leather was used for making shoes, gloves, harnesses, and other articles. There were hunting, trapping, fishing, and a hundred and one other activities, all directed to the one purpose: to provide the necessities and comforts of life for the family.

This picture presents a primitive economic life, an economy of self-help or self-sufficiency, characterized by hard work and a low standard of living. Theoretically, however, it is of great importance in this connection, as it portrays an interesting contrast to our present economy. It is direct acquisition; direct, because under this system goods and services are produced directly by those who consume them. There is no trade, no money, no prices, no marketing, no selling, no buying, and, above all, no unemployment. Production is unhampered by any problem of distribution. The only problem limiting economic advancement is the problem of production. As long as goods can be produced, acquisition is progressing; and the more that can be produced, the more the family will have to enjoy.

2. Indirect Acquisition

Today we have an indirect-acquisition economy, an economy based on specialization and exchange. The goods which we individually produce today are consumed by a multitude of other people, while the goods which we consume are produced by other multitudes. The productive process is so divided among the population that each producer or productive concern is given to produce only one commodity or service in the common weal, one to produce soap, another wheelbarrows, a third razor blades. The duties are so divided that each worker is assigned a most minutely divided task, one to transport coal, one to file papers, one to tighten screws and bolts. We have developed a giant, nationwide, or worldwide, co-operative for the production of one another's goods and services, each producing other people's goods and services and receiving other people's goods and services in return. Practically none of his needs are produced by the individual producer himself. The home has become a place in which to live and sleep alone.

This development, however, has created a situation under which people are dependent on one another even for their barest means of subsistence. No longer can the individual depend on his own strength and skill to provide him with a livelihood. In order to carry on his economic acquisition he must have his specific contribution recognized and exchanged for a value in other people's goods and services. That is, he must be paid in a credit instrument (money) which entitles him to select and withdraw from the general market, or from the common stock of goods produced, all the varieties of goods and services which he needs or desires for his personal use and which he would otherwise have endeavored to produce for himself. And this applies to each and every one of us. The whole national product in the process of distribution must leave the ownership of those who produce it and be returned in the form of free-choice varieties. Speciality ownership must be exchanged for variety ownership. If this exchange could not take place, specialized production would be impractical as a means of acquisition; and we would have to return to a system of producing each our own means of subsistence in order to survive.

The inevitable fact is, of course, that acquisition under our present economy involves two equally important functions, production and distribution (exchange). Under the old self-sufficiency system only one of these functions was required—that of production. When production was accomplished, the acquisition process was complete. Today production alone would be useless, even if brought to enormous proportions, since this would not complete the acquisition process. No one could live on the things which he himself produces. If the one should be left with his nails, the other with his brooms and brushes, the third with his mechanical skill, all would starve, no matter what quantities of these specialities he might produce or possess. Specialized production will benefit us only to the extent that we can exchange. Whenever exchange (distribution) is limited to a percentage of our productive capacity, there is no purpose in producing goods above this limit, since this production, with all the expenses it would incur, would simply burden us with a greater stock of specialities which we could not use.

From this criterion one can easily comprehend why it is possible under the present system to suffer want in the midst of plenty. It is easy to see why the warehouses of the nation might be stacked full of merchandise and food rotting on the ground, while millions cannot afford the necessities of life. It is easy to see why machinery and millions of men might stand idle waiting patiently for the opportunity to produce goods and services, while the nation is in dire need of economic growth to keep pace with communism. It is not, as some people might assume, caused by the lack of resources, human, material, or financial. Nor is it caused by any lack of incentive to produce, nor by any lack of desiderative demand for goods and services. It is caused, indeed, by the sluggishness of exchange, the difficulty of exchanging specialities for varieties, or, as we might say, the difficulty of exchanging specialities for money, the element which gives access to free-choice varieties. And as long as this difficulty persists, men and machinery will stand idle.

There is a great deal of misunderstanding among those who suggest measures for the relief of the present unemployment problem. Many accept the easy *post-hoc-ergo-propter-hoc* assumption that when there is unemployment, the thing to do is to "create jobs," to aid the factors of production by financial, educational or other means, or to urge employers to employ more labor. Whatever merit these suggestions might convey, they apparently support the wrong end of the acquisition process. Urging and abetting people to produce goods and services is like fixing the good tire and leaving the flat one unrepaired. It seems logical that our first concern should be to ensure that the goods produced will come to our benefit, that exchange from specialty to variety is assured, without which specialized production is of no avail. Our problem is not how to produce goods and services, but how to come into interchanged possession of these goods and services. What good would it do to urge people to produce goods, if these goods simply serve to swell their already idle plethora of unusable specialities? If we can ensure that increased production will readily result in increased money income to the producer, more wealth, more luxuries, more comforts and conveniences, more services, more and better homes, we will find no need for urging people to produce. Producers and manufacturers, in fact, are ready at a moment's notice to switch into high gear and employ every man, as soon as exchange is assured.

The problem of how to produce goods and services is undeniably a problem to be considered in any program aimed at increased economic well-being and accelerated growth, especially in an underdeveloped country, but it is not the problem with which we are concerned here. Under a self-sufficiency system, where the members of the family produce their own means of subsistence, the capacity to produce becomes the sole factor accountable for economic welfare. The same is true under communism, where distribution no longer presents a problem. It is logical, also, that as soon as the problem of distribution has finally been conquered in the West, the capacity to produce goods and services under free enterprise, the skill and enthusiasm by which production is pursued, and the mechanical and technological devices by which it is aided, will and must determine our rate of progress toward a higher goal. But, as we have said, this is not now our concern. Our present concern is to enable us to utilize the productive capacity we already possess, to remove the hindrance to production caused by exchange difficulties, and bring the economy up to the performance level at which the capacity to produce will be the determining factor in economic growth.

3. Full Capacity

How serious is the problem of distribution? How great is the loss of output, or how far below capacity is the economy suppressed by the market bottleneck?

It would be difficult to obtain statistical evidence from which a definite answer to this question might be obtained; but one thing can be said for certain, that the problem is often seriously underestimated. Economists oftentimes base their calculation of productivity loss on unemployment figures, which, they point out, register only five or six per cent of the available labor force. This estimate is further minimized by the fact that same economists tend to define a condition of full employment as one which registers an unemployment rate of two or three per cent. If to this we add that in some European countries the rate of unemployment is down to one or two per cent, and also that in some other countries, such as Japan, no unemployment is recorded, we might be led to assume that the Western economy is operating pretty well at full capacity.

The error is caused by the mistake of using unemployment figures alone as a standard for measuring productivity loss, thereby ignoring the greatest cause of this loss, viz., the resistance factor. The problem of distribution may be described as a market resistance or market bottleneck, which hinders the free flow of goods from producer to consumer, or, in other words, which hinders the exchange of goods from speciality to variety; and this resistance does not necessarily result in idleness; rather it leads to the loss of efficiency. Whenever we encounter resistance in any work or activity, our usual discovery is that it requires more than the usual amount of physical energy to produce a given effect, or else that the same amount of physical energy brings a reduced accomplishment. The net result in either case is a lowered standard of efficiency, not necessarily idleness. It would be quite possible for the government of a country to put all the nation's unemployed to work on some non-essential project, such as the carrying of rocks or the cutting of brush, and to pay them at least as much as they now receive in unemployment benefits; but to conclude that we then would have no problem of distribution or that we would then be operating at full capacity would be absurd. Registered unemployment is undoubtedly a tangible evidence of waste, but it is by no means the only evidence of such waste. By far the greatest manifestation of productivity loss is that occasioned by market resistance.

But to corroborate this contention, let us consider the question: What constitutes full capacity, or what circumstances are suited for the full utilization of productive resources, human and material? Naturally, by full capacity we do not mean a condition under which each and every person is compelled to work to the limit of his physical strength; nor do we mean a condition under which mechanization or automation has been brought to its extreme limit. We mean, rather, a condition under which production is unhampered by the exigency of coming into interchanged possession of the goods we produce. There is a limit to productive capacity, human as well as mechanical. In a free democracy manpower is limited to the amount of physical and mental labor which each person by his own free will will choose to contribute to productive activity in pursuit of his own acquisition. Mechanical power is limited to the technological advancement current at any one development stage. Full employment, or full capacity production, must imply that these productive agents are not limited, hindered, restrained, or slowed down by market resistance. It must mean a condition under which goods are being purchased and withdrawn from the market as fast as they are marketed or produced, so that nothing will delay the full utilization of the available resources.

4. Disguised Unemployment

The low rate of economic growth in today's economy is due mainly to the fact that many people, whether classed as unemployed or not, are occupying a non-productive or low-efficiency position, not because they desire to do so, but because market resistance compels them to remain in these positions to make a subsistence. It is, of course, the desire of each person to make his own livelihood independent of charity or relief; and when jobs are scarce and difficult to obtain, there is the tendency for many people to take up any form of activity which promises to bring in the necessary cash, irrespective of whether their chosen pursuits are necessary, productive, desirable, or even legitimate. Mr. A, for instance, decides to pass from door to door selling a commodity, even though this commodity could easily be bought in a neighboring store. His services are not necessary, but he must make a living, so he peddles the commodity. Mr. B, on the other hand, decides to open a store between two other stores selling the same merchandise. This new store is not necessary: it simply splits the sales with the other two; but Mr. B must make a living, so he opens the store. Mr. C, in turn, decides to sell life insurance policies. Now, there may already be a hundred life insurance agents in the field ringing every door bell, and canvassing every potential customer, and another agent is not necessary; but Mr. C thinks that he can exert a little more sales pressure than the rest of them, and that after a few days or weeks he will be able to sell a policy and make a few dollars. Mr. D, again, decides to serve as an advertising agent for a soap company. But this service could hardly be called necessary from a socio-economic point of view; people can easily find enough soap in the stores when they want it. But Mr. D has the same need as every one of us; he must make a living.

This type of activity is disguised unemployment, disguised because the would-be unemployed is doing something, and he is earning enough, perhaps, to support life; yet he is not doing much or anything that will further the economic welfare of the nation. It is a kind of service that could be dispensed with without in any way curtailing the national product or the nation's economic growth. Looked upon from the standpoint of productive capacity, it is economic waste in the same category as unemployment.

A large volume of disguised unemployment is found within distribution, the reason being that this field is usually the easiest to enter. There is no difficulty finding a job which consists in selling things on a commission basis. Oftentimes this is the only position open to the young man who starts out in life.

Another type of disguised unemployment is found within industry and takes the form of excess manpower. Automation is often blamed for robbing workers of their jobs; and there is a strong reluctance on the part of working men to give up their jobs and join the unemployment ranks, even after their duties have been largely replaced by machinery. Thus we find men in industry retained in lower posts or in positions where they have little or nothing to do. This is what is known as featherbedding. There are at present on American railroads alone some 80,000 men who have no work or duty, but who are retained for the sake of relieving unemployment.

A third type of disguised unemployment is found within government services. It is, of course, the desire of governments to relieve the unemployment situation or prevent it from deteriorating, and to this end it employs a variation of means. One way is to retain men in government services, military or otherwise, in greater numbers than these services call for. Another way is to place men on relief work to do manual labor which could be done by machinery in a fraction of the time. Another way again is to retain farmers on the farm in greater numbers than necessary, paying them for not producing, or puchasing their produce and storing it up in government warehouses.

Disguised unemployment number four can be found within the rank and file of the population who are "voluntarily" idle as a result of the difficulty of obtaining employment. Ordinarily, of course, we could not include voluntary idleness in the category of unemployment. This is leisure, not unemployment. The fact is, however, that millions who today are idle would be gainfully employed, were it not for the difficulty of obtaining employment. Yet these people are not classed as unemployed. They are people who feel that they can at least sustain life without the extra earnings which they would have by working, and that even if they were able to gain employment, they would hold down a job which someone else might be in greater need of. Hence they content themselves by remaining idle, despite the lower standard of living which this necessarily entails. During the Second World War in the United States alone some five or six million people not usually on the labor market, married women, older men, students, were drawn into gainful employment. Despite the fact that some nine million men were drawn into the services, the civilian production increased. It would not be surprising if this class alone accounts for as much as ten per cent of the total available labor force.

In the fifth place, there are those who make their support on shady, dishonest or criminal activities, not to mention those who fill our jails. Admittedly we could not hope to abolish crime even under a full-employment economy; but certain it is that unemployment, or the difficulty of obtaining employment, is a strong contributory cause of certain criminal acts pursued for economic gain, especially among youths who crave the good things of life. Unemployment is not only frustrating to those who desire to get ahead in life, to build a home and to raise a family; it is also deleterious to the mind and to the morals. It creates hostility, disloyalty, and disrespect for law and order; and if honest and productive jobs were readily available to those who desire to work, there would in all certainty be fewer people living on criminal acts, and fewer people occupying our jails.

In sixth place are those who today are classified as unemployables, a rather loose term. There is no definite line to be drawn between those who do and those who do not possess the ability or qualification necessary to perform useful work. This line could be drawn higher or lower depending on circumstances or upon the availability of jobs. Today there is a great deal of controversy as to what constitutes unemployability. There are those, of course, who tend to classify all unemployed as unemployables, implying that there is nothing wrong with the system such as it operates, that men are unemployed because they lack the qualifications necessary, or that they do not try hard enough to obtain employment. The argument is that anyone who tries hard enough will find employment. This is equal to saying that if some one loser in a race had run a little faster, he would have won the race. Reason tells us that the harder some people struggle to occupy the available jobs, the harder it will be for others to do so. It is true, indeed, that lack of qualification now exists to do the many high-skilled duties that the present mechanized industry requires; but it is not the lack of qualifications that causes unemployment. On the contrary, it is unemployment that causes the lack of qualifications. This fact was substantiated during the war, when jobs became readily available. Training courses were quickly established in all centers, and millions who previously did not possess the required skill were prepared for and given employment. The reason for the lack of interest in acquiring proficiency today is often that job opportunities are uncertain. In a full employment economy, where jobs were readily available, there would in all certainty be a greater enthusiasm for acquiring required proficiency, not only among those who now are classified as unemployed, but also among those who are suffering from some handicap, physical or mental, and who are supported by charity or other assistance. This means to say that the line between unemployed and unemployables could be drawn lower, leaving a considerable number of extra men and women in the category of unemployed available for employment.

These six classes of disguised unemployment together with what we commonly call unemployment represent the tragedy of human wastage caused by the market bottleneck. It would be difficult to produce exact volume figures for each category; but one thing is certain, that disguised unemployment represents by far the greatest percentage of this wasted manpower. It would not be unrealistic to estimate that in a country with a five-per cent rate of registered unemployment, such as Canada or the United States, there is another twenty-five per cent of disguised unemployment, for a total unemployment of thirty per cent of the available labor force.

Naturally it would not be possible to immediately place all these millions into high-efficiency or high-mechanized industrial jobs, since it would require time to bring mechanization up to date. However, it is anyone's observation that a huge volume of idle industrial capacity already exists, plant and machinery standing idle waiting for an increased demand. The Board of Governors of the Federal Reserve System, through its index of capacity utilization, has found that in many of the major American industries capacity exceeds output by about thirty-five per cent. In conjunction with this finding, Dr. Richard Ruggles, Yale University, and Nancy D. Ruggles, United Nations, estimated that in 1958, for the economy as a whole, output was a good twenty to twenty-five per cent below physical capacity. They also estimated that if all this idle capacity were fully utilized, the United States could produce annually a hundred billion dollars worth of goods and services more than it now does.* If to this we add our own estimate of thirty per cent total unemployment, we get a rough idea of the cost to our social welfare of this greatest-of-all problems in our economic history, the problem of distribution.

To minimize the problem is not in the best interest of our democracy and its future welfare. If we are to remove unemploy-

* Dr. Richard Ruggles, Yale University, and Nancy D. Ruggles, United Nations; Prices, Costs, Demand, and Output in the United States, 1947-57; The Relationship of Prices to Economic Stability and Growth; Government Printing Office, Washington, D. C., 1958.

ment, overt and disguised, we must have a full appreciation of the issues at stake. These astronomical figures of idle men and idle machinery are responsible for a much lower standard of living than we otherwise could enjoy, and the possibilities within our reach are immense. It would not be unreasonable to assume that if distribution was balanced and the economy, given its due time, was brought up to full capacity, we could, for a limited number of years at least, raise our rate of economic growth from the present two or three per cent per year to ten or twelve per cent per year, and that in a matter of five years or so we could increase our GNP by as much as fifty per cent.

It is true, indeed, as someone has wisely stated, that we in America cannot concentrate on filling our own pockets alone and neglecting the millions in other parts of the world who are living in dire poverty. But it is equally true that if we place our economy on a sound, full-capacity basis, we are in a much better position, not only to help these other people in need, but also to spread the ideal of free democracy. To imply that we should refrain from solving our economic problems because other peoples are poorer than we are would not make sense. Our first concern must be to put our own house in order, and other problems will be easier to solve.

5. Guaranteed Markets

Perhaps the most perplexing aspect of the present problem of distribution is that it is unnecessary. There is no logical reason either from a volitional or a practical point of view why it should exist. We might postulate either of two distant possibilities: that unemployment or underutilization of resources is deliberately maintained by some antisocial group supposedly in control of the situation, or (second) that the problem cannot be solved within the framework of our private enterprise economy; but neither of these appears likely. In the first place, there is not, as some people seem to believe, a powerful clique delighting in keeping the economy in a depressed state. Even if some people should desire to maintain poverty and misery, they would not under our competitive system have the power to do so. The employer may appreciate a measure of unemployment in order to have labor readily available, but he could not create unemployment and at the same time gain from this unemployment. There is nothing to be gained from unemployment. The businessman makes profits when men are employed and the economy is booming, not when there is recession or depression. Relief rolls constitute an extra burden on the taxpayer. Governments often stand or fall by their action in dealing with unemployment and would do anything within their constitutions to remove it; and it would be difficult, indeed, to find a single party that would benefit from the perpetuation of the problem.

In the second place, it would be equally difficult to find a single obstacle that could not be overcome in the way of securing full employment or full freedom of acquisition, even within the confines of free enterprise. Such an objective involves little more than the unrestrictive right to produce and to come into possession of the goods produced; and the securing of this right is not an impossibility, whether we have specialization and exchange or whether we have a system of self-help. Today, it is true, we are cooperating in producing our various wants, whereas under the self-sufficiency system each person produced his own wants; but this condition does not justify the forfeiture of our individual right to acquisition. In either case he must sacrifice part of his leisure time in productive work in order to acquire the things he wants. Under the self-sufficiency system he might have worked twelve to fourteen hours a day, because he was unaided by machinery, and the limited amount of wealth he could acquire under these circumstances was worth more to him than the leisure he could have gained by reducing his working hours. Today we are aided by a mass of high-efficiency mechanical devices and can afford to enjoy more leisure; but there is no reason why we should be denied the freedom to choose between wealth and leisure, or why we should be suppressed into a state of poverty because we cannot find recognition for our economic contributions.

Full employment, or full capacity utilization, requires that the market purchases and absorbs all the goods that can be produced, with the population devoting as much time as they desire to productive work, and using as many machines as they can muster. It also requires that the consuming public purchase and withdraw goods from the market at the same rate as deposited, so that goods will pass unhindered through the market from producer to consumer, creating neither glut nor scarcity. In other words, it requires a Balanced Distribution, a condition under which speciality ownership is exchanged for variety ownership (money) at the exact rate at which goods are produced at full capacity; and there is nothing in this exchange that is beyond our power to negotiate, provided that we have a properly functioning market.

There are those, of course, who would express the opinion that if producers and manufacturers in this day of mechanization and automation were guaranteed unlimited markets for goods, there would be more goods produced than we could use. This belief has become commonplace among those who look superficially on the economic problems of the day. The argument is, as we know, that we cannot eat more than so much bread, that we cannot use more than so much soap, and that we cannot wear more than so many shoes. The argument suggests the implication that unemployment is caused by too many goods, or, in other words, that the industrial machine is capable of producing more goods than we can use so that therefore some of us must remain unemployed.

The same idea is expressed in different words by those who speak of "technological unemployment." The idea here is that labor-saving machinery will replace men, who by this action become unemployed. The situation is often emphasized by presenting figures to show how a single machine will do the work of so and so many men, implying that this situation provides a ready explanation of the cause of unemployment. The two ideas could be expressed in common words by saying that the goods needed by the society require less and less human labor to produce on account of the advancement of automation, and that therefore some people must be unemployed.

Needless to say, this kind of reasoning becomes absurd when judged by the criterion of economic welfare. It becomes especially so to the unemployed person himself, who must suffer the consequences of unemployment. He is the person who cannot afford a decent standard of living, because he lacks the many desirable things necessary for such an ideal. He is the person who must solicit public charity for a subsistence, who, perhaps, is evicted from his dwelling because he cannot pay his rent, who, perhaps, must postpone his marriage because he does not own a home or any decent possessions. To him it is not too many goods that is the cause of his troubles, nor is it too many machines with which to produce goods, it is poverty.

The too-many-goods theory would make no more sense even to the person who produced his own means of subsistence under the old self-help system. If his machinery or implements should be sufficiently effective to enable him to produce the needed goods in less than twelve hours, say ten or eight hours, he would certainly not suffer the pangs of starvation as a result. Mechanization in his case would lead to more wealth as well as to more leisure—the natural course of events—not to unemployment and poverty.

It is true that the demand to produce and market goods in today's economy is greater than the demand to purchase and take goods off the market, a condition which appears to favor an overabundance of goods; but the reason for this phenomenon is not that we prefer the first action to the latter. Clearly the very opposite is true. The goods and services which we select and withdraw from the general market constitute our real income and the object of our economic endeavor. They are the things which make our economic and social life healthier, happier, and more abundant. The goods which we produce and deposit in the market, on the other hand, are of no value to us. They constitute the payment which we have to make in return for our chosen wants, and the only reason why we produce them is that we want to come in contact with the multitude of desirable goods and services produced by others. If it should be possible to get access to marketed goods without marketing others in return, specialized production would probably come to a standstill, and the market would be depleted of goods within a matter of hours.

The appearance of "too many goods" in today's market and the consequent cutback of employment and output is caused by an unbalanced distribution. It is caused by the inevitable actuality that under the present pricing system we are called upon to pay a greater value in our own speciality than we receive in free-choice varieties, or, vice versa, that we tend to receive a smaller value in free-choice varieties than we are called upon to return in the form of specialities. If the opposite should be the case and we should receive more of other people's goods and services than we were called upon to deliver of our own, there would be scarcity of marketed goods, and our problem would appear to be shortages and inefficiency of production. With distribution balanced, there could never be too many goods produced, irrespective of any advancement of automation. There could be an oversupply of some commodities and a shortage of others, if prices of individual commodities were not adjusted in compliance with supply and demand; but there could not be general overproduction, since the goods produced in this case would enter the ownership of the producing public interchanged in the precise ratio produced, and the volume of production would be governed by the value equilibrium between wealth and leisure. The idea that too many goods and services would cause unemployment, poverty, and relief rolls under such a condition would be as absurd as the idea that too much money would cause poverty, or that we now have too much wealth and must suffer want.

The guarantee of unrestricted or unlimited markets for goods is entirely within the scope of possibilities. True it requires a measure of balancing and control in order to secure production-consumption balance for each commodity and for all commodities, but it does not involve anything impossible. Generally it involves the task of returning to the producing public the goods which they produce. No person could justly demand much more from the market than what he contributes, and no market, were it ever so well organized, could pay any more or anything else for producers' goods than the goods themselves. It could distribute the papers or credit instruments which entitle the producers to take back with them the goods which they have deposited—less, of course, the cost of exchange.

6. The Market Bottleneck

The present problem of distribution might best be illustrated by means of an analogy. Let us picture, for instance, the market as a giant reservoir or mixer through which all the goods of the nation have to pass to be exchanged from speciality to variety. We shall imagine this reservoir to be circular in form, like a huge cement mixer, and supplied with an opening at the top through which the specialities are entered and an exit at the bottom through which the mixed goods are emptied. Producers, we shall assume, are bringing their various specialities to the machine for the purpose of exchange, depositing them at the top and receiving their share of the mixed varieties at the bottom.

We shall assume, first of all, that we have a balanced distribution, implying that the flow of goods leaving the machine through the exit will always equal that entered at the top, so that the level of contents in the mixer will always remain unchanged. Let us suppose that this level stands at two thirds full. If more goods are entered at the top, more will also leave at the bottom; and if the entry of goods is reduced, the exit is also reduced, so that the two-third level remains.

Producers are free to exchange with the machine as much or as little as they desire. If they want more out of the machine, they must enter more at the top; and if they are content with less of the ready-mixed goods, they are privileged to reduce their deposits.

But let us suppose now that a mechanical disorder manifests itself inside the machine in the form of a dam before the exit, a dam which obstructs the passage of goods leaving the mixer. The balance is upset. The flow of goods leaving the mixer is now smaller than that entering at the top, and the mixer gets full. Producers can no longer find room to deposit their specialities, and their exchange is interrupted. They must have the goods emptying at the bottom in order to subsist; but they can have these goods only if they enter goods at the top in equal—or greater—proportion. But with the exit of goods reduced to a trickle, they must reduce their deposit to the same extent. A struggle results concerning who is to reduce his deposit and who is to have the privilege of proceeding unrestrictedly as before. The question is settled in that each producer resolves by himself that he is the one to have unrestricted exchange; and the outcome is that as soon as the content of the mixer has sunk sufficiently to leave a little room at the top, each producer is struggling to be the one to fill in the little lacuna, and the strongest man has the best chance to succeed. Producers are bringing more and more goods to the machine, piling them up in higher and higher stacks, waiting for an opportunity to squeeze in some of their stocks as soon as there appears a little thinning at the top of the mixer; but many of them are starving beside their stacks of unusable goods.

This picture symbolizes approximately the economic situation in the Western world at this day. Millions of people today are competing to push goods into a market that is already full, and millions of others are competing to push goods out of the market to a population who do not possess the purchasing power with which to buy. And this fruitless struggle is carried on at a frightening cost, not only in monetary values, but also in human wastage. It leaves millions of people unemployed and unable to provide their own means of subsistence and millions of others in an unproductive struggle to push goods. It gives a false appearance of plenty, and has illusioned many people to believe that we have more goods than we can use and that we must in one way or other get rid of them in order to prosper, to give them away or destroy them; that we must export more than we import; that we must limit the use of machinery and go back to hand labor to prevent overproduction; that we must reduce working hours and forbid women and older men to work — all in an effort to reduce the wealth at our disposal. In the meantime, people even on this continent of America are in need of many or most of the commodities and services necessary for a comfortable standard of living. They are spending more than they earn in an effort to obtain the things they need, and are in debt for almost everything they have.

The questions which we must ask ourselves at this time are:

What is the underlying cause of this problem, and what must we do to effect a permanent cure? If we do not know the answer to the first question, we cannot answer the second. We cannot correct an error, or even cure a disease, unless we know what is wrong. We cannot solve the problem of distribution on the precept that we have too many goods, and that we must get rid of them or prevent them from being produced. A patient cannot be brought back to health by treating his outward symptoms alone, by applying a coloring to his face if he looks pale, by pouring cold water over him if he has a fever, or by applying pressure on his heart if his pulse beats too fast; nor can we hope to bring our economy on a sound footing if we cannot see beyond the immediate symptoms of its disease. If the warehouses of the nation are stacked full of goods and people are unemployed and hungry, there must be a cause. What hope do we have of effecting a solution if our efforts consist in a program of distributing more unemployment allowances alone, more assistance, more pain relief, but leaving the cause of the problem untouched? How much confidence can we bestow on a political party or government that promises to solve the problem by pushing more of our goods across the border to some other country, or by storing away more goods in government warehouses, or by attracting more tourists to take away some of our goods, or by placing more men in non-productive occupations, or by supporting a greater and greater army of men in idleness, or by dividing the available work between more people? How can we hope to prosper if we continue a struggle that does not bring us anywhere? How can we hope to win the battle with communism on the economic front if we persistently repeat the same fruitless struggle with the symptoms of our economic disease and each year leave communism a step nearer to victory? How long will we continue to stage this spectacle of futility which can only bring smiles to the faces of our communist adversaries? Is it too early that we should ask ourselves what causes the trouble, and what we must do to effect a permanent cure?

Chapter III

PURCHASING POWER

The problem of distribution, speaking in general terms, is the problem of purchasing the goods and services which we in the Western world produce or have the capacity to produce. If we should ask any person at random how to solve this problem, he would almost certainly say: Create more money; place more money in the hands of the public, and the problem will be solved. This solution appears so self-evident that the answer comes spontaneously. We must have money in order to purchase goods; and with goods stocked up in stores and warehouses out of reach of the consumer and men and machinery waiting for markets, what could be a more likely remedy than an increased volume of money?

Before we subscribe to this panacea, however, let us ask the question: If the problem of distribution could be solved by the simple process of increasing the money volume, why has this not been done already? The problem of distribution has been with us for centuries and has caused more deprivation, more misery, more distress, and more heartache than all the wars in modern history. It has hindered progress toward a richer life, and has kept millions in poverty and discontent. If this problem could have been solved simply by issuing more paper notes or by adding more numbers to people's bank accounts, is it likely that we in this scientific age would stand helpless before such a task? We have been able to split the atom and make bombs that could demolish a city. We have been able to navigate space and send rockets to the moon and to the planets. Would we stand helpless before the task of issuing the papers or the numbers that would enable us to come into possession of the goods we produce, even as free democracy is threatened? It does not seem likely.

1. Definition of Purchasing Power

The fallacy in the not-enough-money argument is caused by the confusion between money and purchasing power, or between an increased money volume and an increased volume of purchasing power. Undoubtedly an appropriate increase in purchasing power would solve the problem of distribution, but an increased money volume would not in any way consummate this increase. An increased money volume would simply raise prices and leave the level of purchasing power no higher than before, except, perhaps, for a very limited duration. We might increase the money volume tenfold or hundredfold, but the purchasing power of the nation would not thereby increase. In 1923 the German Mark was increased a billionfold, but the purchasing power of the nation did not increase. In fact, prices increased at a faster rate than the numerical increase of Mark, so that the purchasing power in the hands of the public registered a gradual decline.

A nation's purchasing power might be defined as its total volume of money, or monetary credit, expressed in terms of the goods and services which this money could buy. An increase in purchasing power could be expressed in terms of the increased volume of goods and services redeemable with the money volume. If, for instance, the money volume was sufficient at a given time to purchase the total national output produced during a six-month period and this was increased to represent eight months, we would say that the purchasing power had been increased.

Increasing the purchasing power of the nation could be done by increasing the numerical volume of money without increasing prices. It could also be done by reducing prices without reducing the numerical volume of money. Alternatively, it could be done by increasing the volume of money more than prices or by reducing prices more than the money volume, or by any other means which would increase monetary credit in relation to prices. It could not be done, however, by increasing money and prices to the same extent, or by reducing prices and money to the same extent, since this would not change the relation between money and prices. Doubling the numerical money volume would not in the least increase our purchasing power if this were accompanied by a like doubling of the price level. We would have twice as many dollars, but each dollar would purchase only half as much as before. Cutting the price level in half would not increase our purchasing power, if this had to be done by eliminating half of our money volume. Each dollar would now purchase twice as much as before, but we would have only half as many dollars.

That an increased money volume would solve the problem of distribution would be correct if this increase should constitute an increased value-volume of money in contradistinction to a numerical volume. Such an increase would be synonymous with an increase in purchasing power.

The money illusion, however, is deeply rooted. Many people will resolve that a dollar is a dollar and that two dollars is twice as much as one dollar, irrespective of price changes. Scientifically it would be inconsistent to say that our monetary savings had increased, if an increased figure of savings did not represent a greater volume of goods and services. It would seem that the least important consideration is the number into which our savings are divided. If we have two pounds of butter in one lump and we proceed to cut this lump in two, we have no more butter than before. Nor would it be logical to say that two hundred dollars is more money than one hundred dollars, if the larger figure does not purchase any more goods and services than the smaller.

Purchasing power, however, must not be confused with money, even in the case that the latter retains a fixed valuation. It would be quite possible to estimate fairly accurately the number of monetary units in existence in a country at any one time, whether or not we include "near money," or securities readily convertible into cash. It would be difficult, on the other hand, to express purchasing power in mathematical terms and make sense. To say that a nation possesses a hundred million dollars of purchasing power would not be logical, since there is no precise limit to the amount of goods and services which can be purchased with a given volume of money during a given period. Our money is a circulating volume. It is not used up in the purchase of goods;

it simply passes from one hand to another and continues to exist, ready to purchase more goods. If there should be a hundred million dollars of monetary credit in existence in a country and the citizens should spend during a given period a hundred million dollars, there would still be one hundred million dollars in existence. The money would simply have passed over to other hands, and perhaps back again. Usually money will pass from consumer to retailer with the purchase of goods. Retailers will hand the money over to wholesalers with the purchasing of supplies. Wholesalers will hand it over to producers and manufacturers, and these again will hand it over to consumers to complete the circuit; but the money, *citeris paribus,* will exist in the same volume as before. This means that a given quantity of money could purchase almost any volume of goods, provided that it circulated fast enough. A hundred million dollars could purchase one hundred million dollars worth of goods in six months, if it made one complete revolution in that time. But it could purchase two hundred million dollars in goods during the same period, if it made two complete revolutions, and it could purchase six hundred million, if it made six revolutions.

Purchasing power might assume either of two different meanings, depending on our choice of definition. It might be defined as the capacity to purchase goods, or it may be defined as the voluntary demand to purchase goods. The first of these definitions, however, would be difficult to attest, since there is no definite limit to the amount of goods and services that a given volume of money could purchase. In this issue we shall accept the latter definition, that is, the demand to purchase goods and services when people are free to spend and save as much or as little as they please. This definition, then, will be synonymous with the term "demand."

But, accepting this definition, it is clear that a given volume of money may have more or less purchasing power depending on its velocity or circulation. If circulation should be brisk, people passing money between them at an accelerated speed, unconcerned with savings, the existing money volume would have greater purchasing power. If there should be an exceptional propensity on the part of the public to save, circulation would slow down, and the purchasing power effectiveness of money would diminish.

This means, also that it would be possible to increase the purchasing power of the nation to some extent without either increasing the numerical volume of money or reducing prices, that is, by creating conditions favorable to spendings. And, as we know, people's propensity to save or spend is affected to a large extent by price movements. When prices are rising, people will want to spend before prices go higher, and the velocity of circulation will increase. When prices are falling, people will endeavor to pile up savings in anticipation of lower prices; and money velocity and purchasing power will suffer.

2. Supply and Demand

Money, or purchasing power, is the element which enables us to come into interchanged possession of the goods we produce, or, as we may express it, which affords power over one another's goods and services. And in this capacity it is the most important determinant of the economic behavior pattern of our society. Whether we have a recession, a depression, a prosperity, or a scarcity condition depends on the existing level or purchasing power relative to capacity; and any rise or drop in this level will change the appearance of the economy. All goods produced under specialization, as we know, must leave our possession as specialities and return to our possession in the form of free-choice varieties, an exchange which can be accomplished only through the medium of purchasing power; and if this purchasing power at free demand purchasing, is insufficient, some potential goods will remain unsold, and some workers will remain unemployed. If purchasing power, at free demand purchasing, is excessive, there will be scarcity of goods and labor shortage. Bring purchasing power to a superabundance, and we will have repudiation of the currency and chaos. Remove purchasing power, and we will be left each with our speciality, unable to come into possession of one another's goods and services, and, consequently, starving. In order that we may enjoy a healthy economy, purchasing power must be meticulously balanced according to capacity. Balanced purchasing power means balanced distribution, which must be the ultimate aim and object of economic planning. If we designate the optimum or balanced level of purchasing power with the number 100, our object must be to establish and maintain the purchasing power index at this figure, never to permit it to rise above or to fall below.

This equilibrium objective between purchasing power and capacity could be expressed in different words by saying that demand must equal supply. But here we encounter two very important questions, viz., What constitutes demand and What constitutes supply? Either of these terms may convey more than one meaning; and if our axiom is to carry truth, we must apply the proper definitions. There is, to be true, a fairly unanimous agreement in economic circles as to the meaning of demand, this being effective demand, or demand with ability to pay. However, we might conceivably interpret demand simply as desiderate demand, that is, the desire to have or come into possession of goods, whether money is available to pay for these goods or not. Quantitatively, the two definitions might be entirely different. A person, for instance, might desire to have a mansion but have money to pay for a shack, or he may desire to have a Cadillac but have money to purchase a bicycle, or he may want a swimming pool but have money enough for a washtub. Naturally, the definition applicable in this connection is effective demand, that is, the demand to purchase goods and services when money is available to pay for them, or the demand to exchange money for goods and services. Accepting our definition of purchasing power, not as the capacity to purchase goods and services, but as the free demand to purchase goods and services, we must conclude that purchasing power and demand express in effect one and the same thing.

There is a much greater controversy surrounding the meaning of "supply." This term might be interpreted either as the actual supply of commodities produced and available for sale or as full-capacity supply, the latter including potential supply suppressed by overt and disguised unemployment. Economists often base their supply-demand deliberations on the former interpretation, a practice which might be appropriate in certain connections. In our case, however, this narrow interpretation of goods available for sale would be entirely inadequate and misleading. We are speaking of the optimum balancing of supply and demand; and the only sensible interpretation of this equilibrium is that which balances demand with full capacity supply, that is, the supply that is made available when people in general have full freedom of acquisition, freedom to choose between wealth-acquisition and leisure, freedom to spend as much time as they desire in productive work, and freedom to utilize all the mechanical devices procurable for maximum output.

The definition of supply as marketed goods only ignores a huge volume of potential supply suppressed by the market bottleneck. It ignores the millions of unemployed who are demanding to exchange their specialities for money. It ignores producers and manufacturers who have idle capacity and who are ready to pour additional supplies on the market as soon as demand permits. This potential output represents supply just as real as that which is already produced. It can be made available at any time that producers and manufacturers find it profitable or purposeful to produce it. It is held in abeyance, because there is no purpose in producing specialities that cannot be exchanged for money.

A plan to balance purchasing power (demand) with existing supplies would not solve the problem of distribution, nor would it mitigate it. The fact is that demand and existing supplies are already fairly well balanced, and would be so under any economic conditions. Producers, manufacturers, and dealers will not continue to stock up inventories much above what they can expect to sell within a reasonable time. When goods do not move, the usual practice is to curtail production and create unemployment. When conditions look exceptionally bright, these producers, manufacturers, and dealers will endeavor to stock up on inventories in anticipation of higher prices, and when conditions look dull and falling prices seem imminent, they will endeavor to sell out and reduce their stocks on hand. This means that existing supplies will generally balance with demand at any stage of the business cycle. It means that even under a severe depression, when half or more of the nation's productive capacity were unemployed on account of the lack of demand, demand and existing supplies would fairly well balance; and if purchasing power should be suppressed to such an extent that only twenty-five per cent of the nation's capacity was utilized, demand and existing supplies would still balance. Needless to say, that this balancing, from a socio-economic point of view, is meaningless and, in this connection, absurd. If a supply-demand equilibrium is to make sense, we must by "supply" mean the free and unrestricted demand to exchange goods and services for money. We must mean, in other words, that the demand to purchase (exchange money for goods and services) must equal the demand to sell (exchange goods and services for money), or that the act of selling will encounter no greater resistance than that of buying.

This does not mean to say that under a condition of demand-capacity equilibrium every commodity produced, of whatever description, can find a ready market. In a changing world where human wants and desires are always shifting in favor of new and better things, where some commodities become obsolete and new commodities and utilities take their place, we can expect some temporary resistance in selling certain commodities and some temporary shortage of others. A commodity that is becoming obsolete will have a tendency to be left unsold in the market, and the price of that commodity must be reduced to discourage its production and also, perhaps, to encourage its consumption. A commodity which is becoming unusually popular will have a tendency to become scarce, and its price must be raised to encourage production and (perhaps) to discourage consumption. These frictional disequilibrium experiences cannot be avoided even under the must delicate balance between overall supply and demand.

Nor could we guarantee that every person could readily find suitable employment in the line in which he desires to work and in the area or location in which he lives, nor even that every employer will find suitable labor whenever and wherever he demands it, even if the overall demand for labor should equal the overall demand for employment. But these imbalances are individual cases which require individual adjustments, whether it concerns commodities or labor. Optimum balance between supply and demand means that the overall demand to purchase goods and employ labor must equal the overall demand to sell goods and secure employment. This ideal purchasing-power balance is what we have designated with the number 100.

3. Symptoms of Overdistribution

But suppose now that we should experience this optimum balance between supply and demand and should proceed to raise or lower the purchasing power level, for instance to 110, 120 or 130, or to 90, 80 or 70, what would happen? A physical scientist who wants to study the behavior of an element under different temperatures will place the element in a test tube and apply various degrees of heat, ranging from below zero centigrade to hundreds of degrees above. In this manner he can tell at what temperature the element changes from a solid to a liquid and from a liquid to a gas and vice versa. It is not quite as easy as that to raise and lower the nation's purchasing power for the sake of studying its impact on the economy. This could be done only by pegging prices at a given level and proceeding to increase or decrease the nation's money volume. However, it would not be necessary to do so, considering that we already have ample empirical evidence of varying levels of purchasing power, past and present. There is no lack of examples of an insufficiency of purchasing power, in the first place, since this has become a general feature of our economy; but we also have examples of an excess of purchasing power, such as during wartime and in countries in which price control is in effect; and it is quite possible from a study of these examples to analyze the general impact of a changing level of purchasing power.

Perhaps the best example of an oversupply of purchasing power is that handed down to us from the Second World War. With price ceilings in effect and with huge government expenditures to finance the war, the purchasing power was brought far above that necessary to balance production and distribution. The result was unmistakable. Goods seemed to disappear overnight. In no time was there rationing of practically everything in the market.

Almost everything that was produced could be sold, and every man and woman who could work could find employment. Nonproductive and low-efficiency jobs were exchanged for productive and high-efficiency employment. Sales pressure was relaxed, and buying pressure was increased.

We may also profitably study the economy in communist countries where price control is in effect. In the Soviet Union, for instance, prices are rigidly controlled by the government and are not affected by changes in demand. The Soviets, however, have been unable to control the volume of credit. With huge government appropriations to industry, and with employers bidding higher and higher wages in an effort to attract labor, the purchasing power has been brought far above the nation's output of consumables, with the result that goods have been scarce and money abundant. And despite the implementation of strong corrective measures, such as heavy taxation, bond issues and other savings schemes as well as increased productivity, this repressed inflation has continued to harass the nation's economy, and one often finds people queued up in front of empty stores waiting for goods to arrive warm from the factories.

An oversupply of purchasing power creates a number of recognizable features, some of which we are well acquainted with from our wartime experience. One of these features is hoarding. When commodities are scarce or threaten to become scarce, people will rush to the stores to buy goods in excess of their normal requirements to escape shortages, a process which greatly aggravates the scarcity condition; and the more essential the commodities concerned, the more serious this panic buying is likely to be. As long as consumers are certain that commodities will be available when needed, nothing extraordinary will happen; but even a wild rumor that goods will be in short supply might be sufficient to activate a process of panic buying and hoarding, reminiscent of the nineteenth-century bank panics.

Another symptom, of course, is rationing. When there is more money in the country than there are goods to buy, the government must endeavor to correct the situation by issuing a new type of currency in the form of ration cards, which limit the purchasing of essential commodities to the actual availability of these items. This ration card issue, then, becomes the real spendable income of the population, since this income can at no time be higher than the goods and services produced, the extra earnings above this limit being compulsory savings.

A third characteristic feature is blackmarketing, the selling of goods above government price ceilings, granted, of course, that excess purchasing power could be maintained only under strict government price control. When purchasing power is excessive, goods are necessarily scarce and difficult to obtain, and the pressure against price ceilings is great. Many consumers would be willing to pay considerably more than the stipulated price, provided that the desirable articles could be obtained; and if price control should be abandoned, prices would soar skyward. Under these conditions many dealers, producers and manufacturers are tempted to get around price ceilings by withholding goods until a higher price is offered. During the Second World War blackmarketing was brought to such an extent that legal action was taken against 26,250 cases in Canada, 73,738 cases in Great Britain, and 259,966 cases in the United States.*

4. Loss of Productivity

A fourth symptom of overdistribution is evidenced in the form of suppressed productive capacity comparable with that of the present. This is a point of great interest in this study, yet one that has not been adequately covered by economic theory, the reason being that it has not provided a serious problem in our free-enterprise environment. Private enterprise is characterized by a low level of purchasing power. The only occasions in our economic history when the purchasing power has been brought up to and above the level of supply-demand balance is during wartime, but these events have been too unsettled to properly evaluate their effect on productivity and economic growth. The fact is, however, that if we should embark on a program of raising the

* Marshall B. Clinard, The Black Market, Rinehart and Company, Inc. New York, 1952, p. 32.

level of purchasing power to indefinite heights, starting from the present insufficiency level, we would find that productivity and capacity utilization would reach its peak at the point of supply-demand balance, after which it would decline in exact ratio with the excess of purchasing power. There would be idle men and idle machinery; and if the same purchasing-power incrementation process should continue, industrial production would eventually be brought practically to a stand-still, and the population would suffer want.

The explanation of this phenomenon is that a superabundance of purchasing power — barring government rationing — would create a market depleted of goods, and that this situation would make specialized production purposeless or, in fact, impractical as a means of acquisition. It would simplify the one part of the acquisition process, exchanging goods and services for money, but it would make the other part (exchanging money for goods and services) almost impossible. The working man would encounter no difficulty finding employment, or exchanging his labor for money, but he would find it purposeless to work for monetary wages, since the money he received would not give him access to the goods and services he needed for his support. Nor would the producer, the manufacturer, or the dealer find any difficulty marketing or selling his merchandise for money, but would find it useless to do so for the same reason. When the market teems with desirable goods and exciting luxuries of all descriptions, the incentive to work and produce for monetary reward is great, but as soon as scarcity appears, this incentive is weakened; and the more difficult it becomes to find the articles needed, the more reluctant producers, manufacturers, and others will be in exchanging their specialities for money.

Looked upon from a sociological point of view, this behavior pattern becomes ironical. It implies that the greater the shortage of goods and services is as compared with the purchasing power available to buy them, the weaker will be the incentive to produce and supplement the deficiency. If the imbalance should be so great that people with bulging pocket books were unable to find goods to buy, few would want to work and produce.

Nor could this ironic behavior be considered anything but natural, in view of the fact that we are living under a system of specialization. The person who works or contributes to economic activity is doing so, not for the goods and services he produces—for these are of little value to him—but for the money he receives, for this element affords him access to the goods and services he needs for his subsistence. But if goods are so scarce that purchasing, or trading of money for goods, is almost impossible, money has lost its value; and the person who already possesses a good supply of ready cash would find it purposeless to work in order to earn more money. He would argue: "Why should I go to work to earn a few extra dollars? I already have an abundance of money which is of no value to me."

The same circumstances are present where the sale of merchandise is concerned. We already know from wartime experiences that when goods are scarce and money plentiful, commodities have a tendency to disappear under the counter. And the reason is obvious. When goods are scarce and difficult to obtain, people will change their minds about selling articles which might at a later date become useful to themselves and which they then might have difficulty obtaining. This constitutes hoarding by producers and dealers themselves. And, naturally, the more difficult it became to obtain the commodities concerned, the more persistent these commodities would be withheld from the goods-hungry public. This means that if the government should proceed to boost the nation's purchasing power to extreme proportions without imposing compulsory labor, rationing, or other emergency measures, industrial collapse and famine would inevitably result.

We might best understand this situation by going to the extreme and supposing that the government should attempt a prodigious munificence by distributing to each man, woman and child a stupendous wealth in paper money, yet stipulate that the price level should remain unchanged. The most likely outcome is that people would quit working and producing. With millions of dollars in their possession few would see the purpose of earning a few extra dollars, which, in any event, would be useless. Nor is it likely that under this condition anyone would desire to work for the sake of exercise or association, since this would be a condition of extreme poverty, not of affluence. There would be an immediate and complete repudiation of the currency, and those who attempted to use their millions to purchase goods, homes, luxuries would find no salesmen. All that they would find would be buyers just as eager as themselves to purchase goods. Merchants, producers, and others who possessed any type of goods would requisition these goods for their own use, or would barter them for other goods more in line with their own requirements. Starvation would result, and people would have to return to self-help in order to survive.

From the same reasoning we can draw the conclusion that any excess of purchasing power, large or small, will adversely affect economic activity and the standard of living. There is an optimum level of purchasing power, a level at which the demand to purchase (exchange money for goods and services) equals the demand to sell (exchange goods and services for money). When the purchasing power is held at this level, supply and demand are at balance, and productivity is at its peak. As soon as the purchasing power is brought above this level, demand increases and supply and productivity decrease; and the further the purchasing power is brought above this balanced level the more the demand is increasing and the more the supply and productivity is decreasing. In figure 1 purchasing power is pictured as a stack of silver dollars which supports the heavy end of a level supplied with pointers. These pointers indicate on a dial what would happen if purchasing power was brought above supply-demand balance. Demand on this purchasing power barometer stands at a figure of 130, while supply and productivity both stand at 70. Should the purchasing power be brought to an extreme, demand would rise towards an indefinite figure of 200, while supply and productivity would decline toward the zero mark.

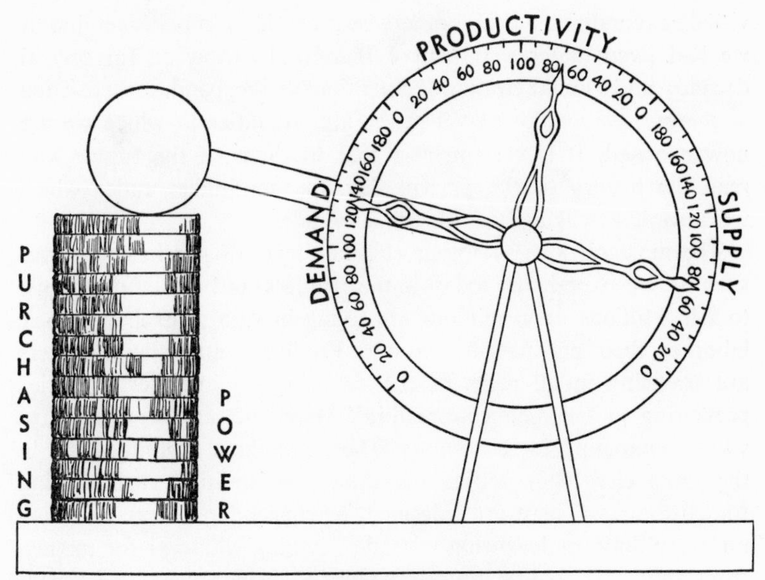

Fig. 1 OVERDISTRIBUTION

5. Symptoms of Underdistribution

What are the symptoms of a low or depressed level of purchasing power, a level at which the demand to sell (exchange goods and services for money) is greater than the demand to purchase (exchange money for goods and services)? It would seem needless, considering our empirical attestations, to answer this question in any degree of detail. For decades and centuries we have experienced an almost constant case of purchasing power deficiency, and the symptoms are meeting us eye to eye everywhere and in every walk of life. However, we have lived with the symptoms so long that we have come to take them for granted. A person who had lived in darkness all his life would consider daylight as something very unnatural. So also, we have lived with unemployment, sales resistance, stocked up inventories, idle capacities, wasted sales efforts, and relief rolls so long that we cannot visualize conditions being otherwise. Yet it is conclusive that if we had lived under a system of Balance Distribution for several decades and should draw our attention to the conditions existing at present, we would marvel at the abnormalities to which we are now exposed. It is certain, also that to those of the future who read the history of the present day, the conditions under which we now live will appear like a fairy tale.

The most obvious symptom of a low level of purchasing power such as we experience today is the fruitless and wasteful struggle to sell. Millions upon millions are trying in vain to exchange their labor or their products for money. Producers and manufacturers are traveling in all parts of the country and in other countries pressuring to sell their commodities. Merchants are present everywhere competing for customers. There are three or four stores in the same city block selling the same commodities, each waiting for customers. There are salesmen, agents and peddlers knocking on every door, endeavoring to trade anything whatever for money, from shoelaces to life insurance policies. Newspapers and magazines are full of advertisements; the air waves are full of advertisements; the cities and streets are full of advertisements; the highways are full of advertisements — all pressuring people to buy. The cost of selling is often higher than the cost of production. Yet the stores and warehouses of the nation are full of merchandise waiting for customers.

The effects of purchasing power deficiency are, of course, more serious at certain times than at others and in certain areas or countries than in others, depending on the degree of deficiency. There is no precise level at which purchasing power deficiency will remain. Some countries may operate at a somewhat higher purchasing power level than others. This level is also higher during boom periods than during periods of depression or recession. Only for short periods during wartime, however, has the purchasing power been brought up to a sufficiency level, or over. At all other times in recent history and in all countries operating under the free enterprise system, the purchasing power has been depressed below the level necessary to ensure production-distribution balance; and it would be possible to measure purchasing power deficiency at a given time in terms of unemployment, idle machinery or other disease manifestations prevailing, since these manifestations are in exact proportion to purchasing power deficiency.

Thus, if we should repeat our test-tube experiment by placing the purchasing power at a supply-demand balance and from this point proceed to lower the purchasing power to various levels by a step progression, we would undoubtedly find answers to many of the phenomena which presently appear on the economic scene in America and in other parts of the Western world. At the balanced level we would find an economy under which the two functions in today's acquisition process, the exchanging of the speciality for money and the exchanging of the money for free-choice varieties, would encounter the least possible resistance. There would be little difficulty in selling goods or finding employment, in the first place, and at the same time there would be little difficulty finding the goods and services desired in exchange for the money. And even though there would be some resistance in individual cases, there would be no more overall resistance to selling than to buying. As we lower the purchasing power level, for instance from the point of 100 to 95, and to 90, and to 80, and to 70, we would find all the symptoms of purchasing power insufficiency which appear on the economic scene today. In the beginning of the process, the symptoms would be mild. Goods would be purchased or withdrawn from the market at a somewhat slower rate than marketed or produced, and inventories would begin to pile up in stores and warehouses or on the manufacturer's premises. Producers, manufacturers, and dealers would realize the need for sales pressure in order to move goods, and the cost of selling would increase. Some plants would curtail production or close down, and some workers would be shifted to lower posts or to sales promotion.

As we lowered the purchasing power level, the symptoms would intensify. The act of selling would become more and more difficult, and high-pressure advertising would eventuate. Production would be further curtailed, and many plants would be closed down. Business failures and bankruptcies would be the order of the day.

Many workers would be thrown out of employment, and these would endeavor to make a living by duplicated or non-productive activities. All the various types of disguised unemployment would develop. The government would institute unemployment relief schemes, or would endeavor to store away surplus stocks, or export them.

All these symptoms — and many others — would appear even before we had suppressed the purchasing power below the level existing at present. If we should continue to suppress the purchasing power, we would reach a situation reminiscent of that existing at the bottom of the depression in 1933. At that time, with twenty-five per cent of the working population unemployed and another twenty-five percent, perhaps, in disguised unemployment, production was down to about fifty per cent of capacity. Unemployed were drifting back to the farm to attempt the task of making a living by the old method of self-help. Others were

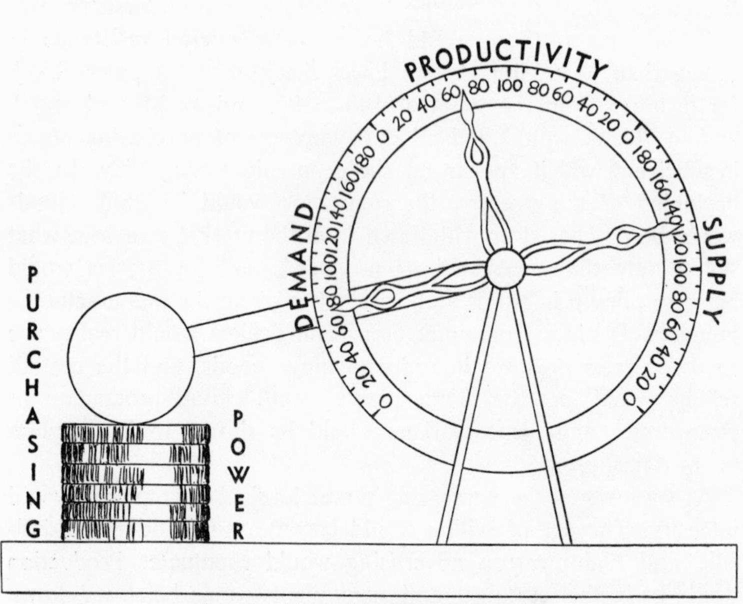

Fig. 2 UNDERDISTRIBUTION

stationed in groups outside every plant, every factory, every mill, and every place where there was some evidence of industrial activity hoping that at least one person from the group would be taken on, and each hoping that he would be the lucky one.

If in spite of this condition we should continue to suppress purchasing power, we would eventually come to the same result as that of bringing the purchasing power to an extreme superabundance. Specialized production would be brought to a standstill, and people would have to return to barter or self-help in order to subsist. Summing up the result of our "test tube" experiment, we would report that the economy would behave generally the same whether we raised the purchasing power above supply-demand balance or lowered it below this level. Specialized production would gradually decline in both cases until people were forced back to self-sufficiency. Figure 2 indicates approximately our present dilemma.

6. Balanced Distribution

It will be clear to anyone who can reason that we cannot solve the present problem of unemployment by renewing our efforts to "create work," to dump goods on some other country to create markets, to establish nonproductive jobs to prevent overproduction, or go back to hand labor. The argument that automation is the cause of unemployment makes about as much sense as the saying that too many goods causes poverty. There is a great lack of logical reasoning on the part of many people who attempt to solve the present problem. Oftentimes the matter is dealt with as if "work" was the end product of our economic endeavor and as if goods were the means to this end. Unemployment is not a problem of how to find enough work, but how to come into possession of the goods and services we need for our support and our enjoyment. It is a hindrance or an obstacle to economic acquisition, and it would be absurd to assume that automation or mechanization should constitute an obstacle to economic acquisition. What the unemployed person wants and, as a matter of fact, what any one person wants concomitant with his quest for employment and economic satisfaction is not necessarily work but purchasing power, the element which gives access to goods and services; and any increase in public purchasing power would reduce the demand for employment, even as it would increase the demand for goods and services in a duel bid to effect supply-demand balance.

But in order that we may fully appreciate this vital economic behavior pattern, let us consider what would be the most probable public reaction to an increased volume of purchasing power. Suppose, for instance, that the government should undertake to issue and distribute, let us say, one hundred dollars of new money to each and every person in the country, assuming also that prices thereby did not increase to counteract the credit expansion. Naturally, to arrive at a reasonable corollary of such a munificence, we would have to base our estimate on the impact on the average recipient, not on that on any one recipient, since the immediate monetary needs of individuals will differ widely between savings, spendings, investments, etc. Generally, there would be an increase in both savings and spendings. Some people, undoubtedly, would immediately spend the extra money on something that they desired, or would make a downpayment on some article of their choice. Others would simply add the new money to their savings, with little or no increase in spendings. Others, again, would use the additional cash to retire a debt, or to make a payment on a credit arrangement or mortgage, or to invest in some security. Overall, however, there would be a moderate increase in the demand for goods with a consequent increase in employment and output. Since the money volume would increase, there would probably be a reduction in interest rates.

But at the same time this increase in purchasing power would reduce the demand for employment in concordance with the law that after a person is in possession of a given amount of wealth any addition to this wealth will have a reduced value and will be outweighed by the value of the leisure which must be sacrificed to procure it. Naturally, the people would be few, indeed, who in possession of one hundred dollars would feel rich enough to quit work. Some people, in fact, would continue working even if presented with tens of thousands, or with so much money that their monetary demands were satisfied, because they find their job agreeable, and they like the association of other people, which they would miss, perhaps, by remaining idle. There are those, however, who would grab any opportunity to quit work, even in possession of as little as one hundred dollars. They are especially those who find their job unpleasant and who desire to gamble for a better position or for an enterprise of their own, but also those who are "allergic" to any kind of savings, for instance those who take to drink and who would make the best excuse to go for a spree. The inevitable outcome of the money increment, therefore, would be an increase in the demand for labor commensurate with the increase in the demand for goods and services and, at the same time, a reduction in the demand for employment.

But suppose now that we undertake to increase the money volume, not with one hundred dollars, but with one thousand dollars per person, or four thousand dollars per family of four, without an increase in prices. Obviously the same general public response would be forthcoming, only much more pronounced than in the case of the one hundred dollars. A much greater number of people would now withdraw their demand for employment. If, for instance, there had been before the purchasing power increment five million unemployed, it is possible that in possession of the thousand dollars one million of these unemployed would withdraw their application for employment, and would no longer be on the labor market. At the same time another million workers might quit their jobs, so that when these had been replaced, there would be only three million unemployed. But, naturally, with this more generous increase in purchasing power there would be a substantial increase in demand for goods and services of all description, new cars, homes, luxuries, capital investments, sufficient, perhaps, to absorb the remaining unemployed and also to call attention to the need for greater efficiency, for discontinuing unnecessary or unproductive work and for relocating excess workers in highly productive positions in a bid to reduce disguised unemployment. Yet shortages of goods as well as labor might be in evidence.

If now we should boost the purchasing power allowance to $10,000, we would bring disaster. Four million out of the five million unemployed, perhaps, would no longer be available for work. Another five or ten million workers would quit their jobs. Industry would already be paralyzed by a labor shortage in the wake of an exploding demand. Instead of exerting themselves in finding employment, people would concentrate on how to find the goods and services to purchase; but, alas, the stores would close, and the money would be repudiated. This means, of course, that whereas an increase in purchasing power is imperative for a healthy future economy, an excess of purchasing power would bring another evil just as harmful as that of the shortage to which we are now exposed.

The "create work" policy which is often suggested today as a cure for unemployment is a futile botchery. The volume of unem-

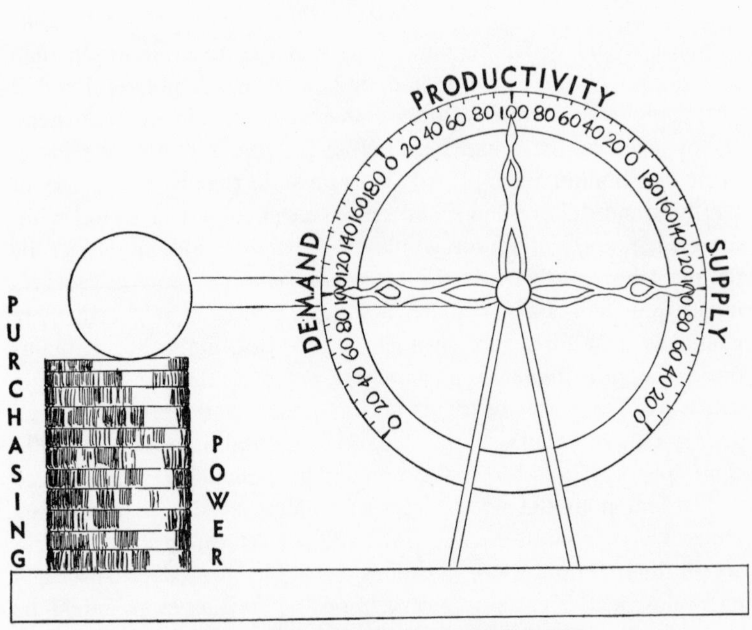

Fig. 3 BALANCED DISTRIBUTION

ployment in any country is not governed by our efforts to advocate production and employment. It is governed, indeed, by the level of purchasing power, and any change in this level will inversely change the volume of unemployment. Today the demand for employment is greater than the demand for labor, but this is because our level of purchasing power is low. Raise this level sufficiently and supply and demand of labor as well as of goods will be brought to an equilibrium. Raise it to an excess and there will be shortage of labor as well as goods. Purchasing power holds the key to the problem of distribution. When the purchasing power is properly balanced, the economy is at the peak of performance. Goods will flow freely through the market from producer to consumer, and production is unhampered by the exigency of exchange. The proper balancing of purchasing power provides the foundation upon which our economy must operate. It will not remove all economic ills, but it will solve the problem of distribution which now lies at the root of our troubles. It will remove the market bottleneck and ensure that goods are purchased and withdrawn from the market as fast as they are produced and marketed; and until we have successfully attained this vital economic equilibrium, no other effort aimed at improving economic conditions is going to do much good.

Chapter IV

PRICES AND SALES RESISTANCE

How do we establish Balanced Distribution? How do we raise and control the nation's purchasing power? Is it possible under free enterprise to increase the present purchasing power to a sufficiency or balanced level and to maintain it permanently in this position? On these questions rest the fate of our free enterprise system. If we fail to control and balance the level of purchasing power, our free democracy may succumb under the pressure of communism. If we succeed, we will enjoy free enterprise at its best, an economy operating at full capacity, yet free from the uncertainties and vicissitudes of the present.

1. The Value-Volume of Credit

There is one thing we can say for certain in reply to these questions, that is, that we cannot supplement the present insufficiency of purchasing power through the limited control potential we now possess. More specifically, we cannot increase or control the purchasing power of the nation by controlling the numerical volume of credit alone, leaving the value volume to take care of itself. As we have already said, the numerical credit volume of the nation could be multiplied a billionfold yet possess no greater purchasing value than before. Any attempt to control purchasing power by controlling the number of credit units alone would be as futile as to attempt to control the distribution of goods by prescribing the number of baskets to be distributed but making no provision for the amount of goods to be placed in these baskets. There are two equally important factors determining the volume of purchasing power in the hands of the public, viz., the number of credit units and the goods value of these units, and no attempt to control purchasing power would ever be successful without the control of both of these factors.

At this day the government has the power to control the numerical volume of credit in the nation, but it has no power to control the value of this credit. The value is governed by price determination which is outside of present government jurisdiction. Consequently the purchasing power of the nation is governed by those in control of prices. Increasing the number of credit units in the country would be the easiest of all tasks. It could be done simply by the signing of a number of checks by a government representative. But to do so would have little or no overall value. It would increase purchasing power for a temporary period until prices had had time to respond, but it would be no more successful than that of attempting to make a permanent heap of water on the sea. Nor would a second or third attempt be any more successful, since each time the credit volume was increased, a corresponding rise in prices would manifest itself to nullify the intended effect. It would be equally possible to effect a temporary reduction in purchasing power by reducing the credit volume, but this again would last only until prices had dropped and restored the purchasing power to its former level.

It seems logical that the first step in any plan to control and balance the nation's purchasing power must be to establish a fixed standard of value, that is, a price level not affected by the volume of credit, and from this point proceed to control the numerical credit volume. A bucket without a bottom will not fill up, for anything that is poured in through the top will pour out through the bottom. But if the bucket is supplied with a bottom, any material poured in will remain, and the bucket will fill up. Similarly, it would be useless for the government to pour credit into the hands of the public, for any increase in credit would be met with a corresponding increase in prices, and the purchasing power would be no greater than before. But if we establish a fixed price level, or fixed standard of value, any increase in the credit volume will constitute an actual increase in purchasing power.

2. The Goods Unit

The act of pricing may be understood as the process of divisioning goods into equal units each representing a standard unit of value. The raising of prices may be understood as the redivisioning of goods into more and smaller units, while the lowering of prices may be understood as the redivisioning of goods into fewer and larger units. A credit unit, however, whether it be in the form of a paper note or a digit in a bank's ledger, cannot give access to more than one unit of goods, irrespective of the size or value of this unit. It can confer on the bearer the clear title to one price unit of goods or the power to redeem one unit of price and set the goods free. The promise which might reasonably be placed on the face of a dollar note might read as follows: This note entitles the bearer to the free choice of goods in the National Market up to the price of One Dollar, or this note is legal tender for goods in the National Market up to the price of One Dollar, or this note is redeemable in goods in the National Market up to the price of One Dollar. But whatever the exact wording may be, one thing is clear; that the note cannot command any power except that of redeeming price, whatever this price may be.

It is evident that this promise in itself is not sufficient to give the bearer the required assurance of a value in goods and services. It is a promise which confers on him a definite right to claim one price unit of goods, but which does not give any assurance of the size or value of this unit. The credit unit is simply a number, no more and no less, and the value of this unit is governed entirely by the forces that determine prices. If these forces are reliable and the price level remains fixed, the credit unit will carry the highest assurance of economic value that could possibly be bestowed on a monetary unit. But if price determination is haphazard and unreliable, the right to redeem a unit of price will be an uncertain privilege.

But in order to illustrate this situation, let us suppose that we conduct an inventory of all the merchandise contained in a store and find that the aggregate price of these merchandise amounts to $10,000. Let us suppose, also, that these goods are of such consistency that they can easily be divided into small units. Accordingly, we could divide these goods into 10,000 little units — or piles — of goods, each representing a standard unit of value. A dollar note, then, would constitute a clear title to one of these units. Ten thousand dollars would purchase the entire stock.

But suppose now that prices should rise so that the total price of these same merchandise would register $12,000. Accordingly, we would now have 12,000 little piles of goods instead of the original 10,000, each being proportionately smaller. Yet a dollar note would still entitle the bearer to only one unit. Ten thousand dollars would still entitle the bearer or bearers to only 10,000 units, leaving 2,000 units to which the bearers of the 10,000 dollars were originally entitled.

Or suppose that the prices should continue to rise until the total price quotations of these same merchandise would reach $20,000. There would now be 20,000 little units of goods after the redividing process was complete, each being only half the size of the original. Yet a dollar note would still entitle the bearer to only one unit, and 10,000 dollars would still purchase only 10,000 units, or half of the goods to which it previously conferred title. The creditors, even though they possess the same number of credit units, would have only one half of their original purchasing power. The storekeeper, by doubling the price of his merchandise, would have cut the purchasing power in half.

If, on the other hand, the price of this merchandise should drop from $10,000 to $8,000, we would have a standard unit larger than the original. Lowering the price from $10,000 to $8,000 could be understood as the process of using 2,000 units, or piles, to add to the remaining 8,000, making each unit larger than before. Yet a dollar note would still purchase one unit. Ten thousand dollars would now purchase the whole stock of merchandise, and there would still be 2,000 dollars left to purchase additional goods.

3. Competitive Control of Purchasing Power

The contention that the government is in control of the nation's money volume is true only in so far as we refer to numbers alone, a consideration which is of lesser importance. If we confer on credit the quality definition it justly deserves, the quality of serving as a title to goods and services, we must admit that the prerogative of credit control is bestowed mainly on those who control prices. Suppose, for instance, that the aggregate price of all the goods in the market at a given time should amount to 80 billion dollars and that the numerical volume of credit is also 80 billion dollars. Consequently, the credit volume would at this moment be sufficient to purchase and withdraw from the market the full 80 billion price units of goods. But suppose now that prices should increase to 100 billions for the same marketed goods. Commonly we would say that the credit volume remains the same; that prices only have risen. But this is plausible only if we think in terms of numbers alone. It will seem equally plausible that the credit volume has been reduced by twenty per cent, since this volume is now sufficient to purchase only eighty per cent of the marketed goods. If prices should rise to 160 billions, the credit of the nation would be down to fifty per cent of its original volume.

It is evident from all angles of reasoning that those who control prices — and this includes each and every one of us who has some goods and services to sell — are responsible for the present insufficiency of purchasing power, and that only through a change in this pricing policy can we hope to supplement this deficiency. Credit expansion alone can do nothing toward this objective. All we could do through credit manipulation is to raise or lower prices with no beneficial effect on the nation's purchasing power. But it seems reasonable that the proper volume of credit to keep in circulation under the present system is that which maintains a reasonably stable price level. In no way, however, is the present shortage of purchasing power due to any presupposed deficiency of credit units which could be corrected by means of credit expansion. It would seem more likely, on the contrary, that the credit volume is already overabundant, judging from the fact that prices are registering a continually upward climb. Increasing the nominal credit volume would simply raise prices at a faster rate without in any way relieving the deficiency of purchasing power.

Purchasing power deficiency is accounted for by the fact that the numerical volume of price is too great in relation to the numerical volume of credit. Price is the element which ties goods in the market; credit is the element which releases goods. Each unit of price placed on goods in the market requires a unit of credit to redeem before the goods so priced are set free. No one can withdraw anything from the market without first redeeming or promising to redeem the price with credit in the same numerical volume. Obviously, if we are to be able to withdraw goods from the market at the rate at which we deposit or can deposit, we must create credit at the same rate as we create price.

The government is quite capable of creating the element which releases goods, but it cannot under the present system prevent the producing and distributing public from creating the element which ties goods, with the result that goods will always be tied out of reach of the existing credit. If the government should attempt to close the gap between price and credit by expanding the credit volume, the public would quickly respond by increasing the goods-tying element of price; and the goods would be as far out of reach as before.

The power to increase or control purchasing power lies with those who are in control of prices. Price control holds the key to purchasing power sufficiency. If the public should refrain from raising prices in spite of an expanding credit volume, the gap between price and credit would soon be closed, and distribution would be balanced—or overbalanced. If care was not taken under this condition, the purchasing power could be brought to extreme proportions. If the credit volume was doubled without any change in prices, purchasing power would also double. If the credit volume should be doubled again, there would be four times as much money in circulation as before.

It would be possible, also, by means of increasing prices, to reduce the purchasing power to almost any level of deficiency. If prices were doubled without any change in the numerical volume of credit, there would be only half as much money or purchasing power left. If prices should double again, there would be only one quarter of the original money left in circulation, ad infinitum. Thus, whereas the authority in control of credit alone has no power either to increase or decrease purchasing power, the authority in control of credit and prices, whatever it be, could quite easily place more purchasing power in the hands of the public as well as wrest this power away from them.

4. The Purchasing Power Squeeze

At this time let us ask a question which is of the most crucial importance in this enquiry. Why is it that we who are in control of prices as well as purchasing power should exert our best efforts to wrest this purchasing power out of our own hands by maximizing prices? Considering that each and every one of us is struggling to come into possession of money with which to purchase the things we need, why should we conduct a war against purchasing power by tying the goods out of our own reach? Why should we frustrate all government efforts to increase purchasing power by hurriedly raising the price tags so as to keep this purchasing power constantly insufficient? We have the power to solve the problem of distribution and dispel any fear of communist competition, simply by the enviable task of placing more money in our own pockets, yet we do everything in our power to aggravate the problem and prevent it from being solved by forcing money out of our own possession. Why?

The answer is, of course, that each person (company, corporation) is acting in his own personal interest, and his interest is to sell at the highest possible price. And even if he is conscious that this maximizing of prices is not in the best interest of society as a whole, he could do little about it. If he should undertake to lower the price of his own speciality, he would be the one to suffer the loss. The lowering of the price of any one person's (company's, corporation's) speciality would affect the price level so little that the effect on the purchasing power would be negligible. But even if it should be sufficient to be noticed, the person selling the speciality would be the least likely to benefit, since he may not be dependent on purchasing his own speciality. He would benefit from a lower price of other people's goods and services which he is dependent on buying, but the more he can get for his own, the better. With this situation in mind, each person (firm, company, corporation) must endeavor his best to sell at the highest possible price, irrespective of its effect on the nation's economy. He has no other choice.

The circumstances under which we live are such that each person, in order to further his own personal interest, must endeavor to be a little ahead of his fellow men in the matter of pricing. If a person could raise his own price with as little as two per cent without others doing the same, that is, without the price level rising, and still sell his speciality, he would make a personal gain. And to many people such a nominal rise would be of great importance. A dealer, for instance, who purchases goods at a given price and sells them at a somewhat higher price may have only a very small per cent profit that he can call his own net income, perhaps only two or three per cent; and if he could raise his price by only this much and still sell his merchandise, he might double his personal income. The same nominal reduction in his price might wipe out his entire income.

But if now all other people should also raise their prices (increase the price level) by two per cent, the gain would be neutralized. The person who then had raised his price by only two per cent would be no better off than before. He would have $102 instead of $100, but the goods which formerly cost $100 would now cost $102, so his real income would remain precisely the same. If, however, he could raise his price by four per cent while others increased their price by only two per cent, he would make a personal gain. He would make a gain, also, if the price level rose by four per cent, provided that he then could raise his price by six per cent and still sell his commodities. Again, he would make a gain if the price level dropped by two per cent, provided that he then could still sell his speciality at the same price as before. He would also profit if he reduced his price by two per cent, provided that others reduced their prices by four per cent.

On the contrary, a person who was left behind with his prices would suffer a loss. If the price level should rise by two per cent and he still was compelled to sell his commodities for the same price as before, his personal profit might be wiped out, and he may be forced out of business. The same would be the case if the price level should remain stable and he should be compelled to reduce the price of his commodities in order to sell. No one would benefit from a higher price level if all prices, rates and dues, were raised to the same extent, nor would anyone suffer a loss from a lower price level if all prices, rates and dues, were reduced to the same extent; but the person who can raise his price a little more than others or lower his price a little less than others and still sell his commodities will make a personal gain, while the person who is compelled to lower his price more than others or raise his price less than others will suffer a loss. This means that in order to do what is best for himself each must struggle to be a step ahead of the other fellow, for "devil take the hindmost." Each must endeavor to raise his price a little more or a little faster than others when prices are rising and to reduce his prices a little less or a little slower than others when prices are dropping. But considering that this ambition occupies the mind of each person, each firm, each company, each corporation, each industrial and distributive unit, we can easily realize the outcome. It is a struggle aimed at the acquisition of purchasing power but which in effect works to force this purchasing power out of existence.

We might illustrate this unfortunate circumstance by an example. Suppose that there are ten industries of equal importance within the economy, and that one of these industries should press for and receive an increase in its price of ten per cent, reflecting in an increase in all wages, salaries, dividends and profits within that industry to the same extent. Consequently, the price level has now risen by one per cent; and those who have received the raise are nine per cent better off than they were before, while those in the remaining nine industries have suffered a loss of one per cent through the reduced money values. But suppose that a second industry also receives a raise of ten per cent. The two industries having received the raise will now be eight per cent better off than they were before, while the remaining eight have suffered a loss of two per cent. When five of the industries have received the raise of ten per cent, these industries will have made a net gain of five per cent, while the remaining five would have lost five per cent through the increased price level. When all the industries have received the raise, they will be back where they started from, with no gain and no loss of income to anyone. The only thing that has happened is that the purchasing power (or savings) in the hands of all concerned, *ceteris paribus,* has been reduced by about nine per cent.

But suppose now that the first industry, realizing that its gain has been wiped out, should proceed to demand and receive an additional raise of ten per cent, and that this should cause a chain reaction which would raise the price in all industries with another ten per cent. There would still be no increase in real earnings to anyone concerned, since the twenty per cent increase in numerical incomes has been canceled out by the reduced money values. The only change would still be an additional drop in purchasing power or savings, other things being the same. If this process should continue until all wages, salaries, profits, and dividends had doubled, the purchasing power in the hands of the public would have been cut in half, but the real incomes would still be no greater than they were originally. Real incomes can increase only by an increase in production, coupled with a properly functioning system of distribution. This struggle for higher prices and higher wages does not in itself increase incomes. The only effect it has on the nation's economy is a strangulation of the purchasing power which, in turn, produces sales resistance and unemployment. The only person who can hope to gain by the struggle is the one who can force his way a little ahead of his fellow men and who, incidentally, has contributed the greatest share to the suppression of the nation's purchasing power.

We often hear the opinion expressed that labor is to blame for pressing exorbitant wage demands, or that manufacturers are to blame for raking off huge profits, or that dealers are to blame for wedging up the cost of living, or that bankers are to blame for demanding high interest rates. The fact is that all are human beings motivated by the same desire to do what seems best for themselves; and as long as there are no socially recognized standards for determining prices, each is going to press for the highest price that he is able to exact. Nor would it be fair to expect that anyone should do otherwise. Price control is the responsibility of the government, or public representative, not that of the individual.

5. Sales Resistance

Why is it, we may ask, that prices do not register a greater and more persistent rise in view of the relentless pressure for higher prices? Why is it that the price level sometimes remains stable, or drops? What restraining factor is present in preventing prices from continuing their upward climb?

The answer to these questions is self-evident, considering the effect of rising prices on the nation's purchasing power. Each rise in prices, *ceteris paribus,* will reduce purchasing power and make it more difficult to sell. If prices should continue to rise without a proportionate increase in credit, the purchasing of the nation would continue to decline. The time comes, naturally, when sales resistance becomes too great and too many sales are lost. Producers, manufacturers, and dealers will weigh between two alternatives: to sell more at a lower price or less at a higher price. They will do everything in their power to sell at the higher price, and will sustain some loss of sales and some curtailment of production; but when all sales efforts have been exhausted and unsold goods are piling up, they will consider modifying their price demands. However, if sales resistance should ease off by an increase in the credit volume or by any other agent, they would quickly take advantage of the situation and raise prices in an effort to boost profits. And this price rise would continue until the purchasing power had been brought down to the same level as before, and the same sales resistance was again experienced. Prices under our free-for-all pricing system are governed by sales resistance. Whenever it becomes less difficult to sell, prices will rise; and whenever it becomes unusually difficult to sell, prices will drop. When the level of sales resistance remains constant, prices will also stabilize.

From this reasoning we arrive at the inevitable conclusion that the present problem of distribution cannot be solved without the implementation of price control. This conclusion is inexorable from whatever angle we approach the problem. With the implementation of price control it will be possible by means of increasing the credit volume to bring the purchasing power to any level desirable. Without price control it appears hopeless to find any avenue that could lead to a possible solution. To solve the problem of distribution we must bring the nation's purchasing power up to a level at which overall demand will balance with overall supply; that is, we must remove sales resistance. But without price control there is no possibility of doing so, because any action whatsoever that would remove or even alleviate the intensity of sales resistance would raise prices and frustrate the effectiveness of the action. No plan of action would assist us in solving the problem of distribution unless it relieved sales resistance and made it easier for people to find market and employment, but any action that relieved sales resistance would raise prices until the same sales resistance was again experienced. *Sales resistance under our free pricing system will always tend to remain at a fixed level or will tend to return to this level whenever some disturbance has temporarily brought it out of its center of gravity.* This is what we will call the Law of Sales Resistance, a law which we cannot escape as long as private price competition prevails.

This law testifies to the hopelessness of finding a solution to the present problem without the benefit of price control. It indicates that we must have difficulty in selling or finding markets and jobs. If not, prices would rise until such difficulty was experienced. Purchasing power deficiency and sales resistance are inescapable in any country in which the individual is free to do what seems best for himself, even though the problem may be more or less severe in different countries and under different circumstances depending on public sentiment, public appeals or otherwise. In a country such as Canada or the United States where the price struggle is of average or greater than average intensity, any prospect of winning the battle against purchasing power deficiency without price control must be counted out. There are two projects which might be considered as a possible remedy, namely, inflating the currency of the country or speeding up the currency already in circulation, but neither of these seems even worthy of trying.

Credit inflation would undoubtedly create a temporary boost in purchasing power. This is obvious for two reasons: it would place more money in the hands of the public before prices had had time to rise and, second, it would tend to speed circulation concomitant with people's propensity to spend in times of credit inflation and rising prices. To be sufficient to supplement the shortage of purchasing power, however, an inflation would have to be substantial. It would have to be sufficient to raise prices at a fairly rapid rate. A moderate inflation which permitted only a three or four points per year rise in the price index would have little or no effect on the economy. In fact, this is what we already have today. An attempt to bring purchasing power up to or near the level of balance by means of credit inflation would cause a galloping inflation of prices; but since this price inflation would counteract the increase in credit, it would be necessary for the government to continue credit inflation at an ever increasing speed with the inevitable sequel of final and complete repudiation. The benefits derived from credit inflation, therefore, would be short-lived. It would last only until the money system had been brought to the brink of collapse, after which chaos would reign.

But a plan to speed circulation would possess an even slimmer chance of doing any good. It would be useless whether it was capable of being accomplished or not. Undoubtedly, an increased velocity of circulation would increase the demand for goods and services and ease market resistance. It would have precisely the same effect on sales and markets as an increased credit volume. Money, as we have said, is not used up in the purchase of goods; it simply circulates from person to person and from company to company, and could purchase a great deal more goods and services if it made a more rapid turnover. A doubling of the velocity of circulation would have the same effect on purchases as a doubling of the credit volume with velocity remaining the same.

Our success in bringing such a velocity-acceleration plan into effect, however, would be contingent on our ability to make people purchase more goods and services than they now do, or to pass money between them at an increased speed. In other words, it would be contingent on our ability to make people increase their spendings in relation to their savings or, vice versa, to reduce their savings in relation to their spendings. And to accomplish this objective we would have to launch a vigorous advertising campaign to make people purchase more goods. But when we consider the fact that the nation is already full of advertisers and salesmen and agents pressuring people to buy, we must conclude that an additional campaign to push goods could hardly be counted on to bring much success. If all the sales pressure with which we now are being bombarded is incapable of making us purchase goods, it would seem unreasonable to assume that a little more of the same pressure would bring the desired result.

But even if we by means of a vigorous sales campaign should be able to make people pass money from one to another at a greater rate of speed and purchase more goods, all that we would accomplish is to cause a temporary easing of sales resistance with the inevitable consequence of rising prices. We would accomplish the same objective as if we had inflated the currency, with that difference, of course, that we would now have a reduced value volume of money. We would have the same number of dollars, but each dollar would purchase a smaller amount of goods. If despite of this reduction in the money volume we should be able to induce people to continue speeding up the money circulation, we would cause further easing of sales resistance and further increases in prices; and the money volume would be on its way to extinction.

6. Futile Alternatives

There is a great deal of public misconception about what causes prices to rise. Many people, apparently, take for granted that prices are governed by the volume of money in existence instead of the utilization or effectiveness of this money in the purchase of goods. Concomitant with this criterion, they have suggested that instead of inflating the money volume, the money already in circulation should be made to do more work by circulating faster, on the hypothesis, perhaps, that prices then would not rise. But this suggestion is ridiculous. Prices will rise when demand increases and producers, manufacturers and dealers find it less difficult to unload their stocks of merchandise on the consuming public. These sellers do not speculate on what has caused the increased demand, whether it has been precipitated by an increased money volume or by an increased velocity of circulation. An increased money volume would not cause prices to rise if at the same time circulation should slow down to counteract the increase. In fact, it would be possible to double the money volume without causing a rise in prices, provided that circulation should then slow down to half its usual speed. For the same reason, it would be possible to activate a considerable rise in prices without any increase in the credit volume, that is, by increasing the velocity of circulation. Prices will rise whenever demand increases sufficient to ease sales resistance and will cease rising when the required difficulty in selling is again experienced.

There are others who have suggested that the money volume should be increased but that it should be done in such a way that it did not inflate prices. Conscious that an increased consumer demand would increase prices, they have suggested that the new money should be given to producers to defray cost, or to dealers to aid in stockpiling, or to investors to encourage capital expansion, or to local government bodies for public works programs, or to foreign countries, or to pensioners, or to someone and in some manner that it did not raise prices. Logical reasoning tells us that any increase in the money volume that did not relieve sales resistance and make it easier for people to find markets and jobs would have no beneficial effect on the problem of distribution; and if it did relieve sales resistance, it would cause a rise in prices which would frustrate the benefits intended.

There are others again who realize the need for increased public purchasing power but who are against the idea of increasing the money supply, knowing that this would inflate prices. They suggest that the increased purchasing power should come from deficit financing, or from government banks, or from low-interest loans, or from commercial bank loans, or from export surpluses, or from private individuals, or from investment companies, or from some one source or another, except from the central bank or the mint. This constitutes another futile search for a solution to the problem of money scarcity, a search for a kind of money that does not raise prices. Any person who can reason will realize that a monetary increment is not greatly different whether it comes from a government loan or from a private loan or from a foreign country or from any other source. Nor will it matter much whether it is "new" money or "old" money, or whether it is paper money or checking account money or metallic money, or even whether it is large notes or small notes or square notes or oblong notes. What matters is whether the addition to the outstanding credit volume is sufficient to increase purchasing power and demand; and if it is, it will cause a rise in prices which will neutralize the benefit of the increase. And if it is not sufficient to raise prices, it will be of no benefit to the cause intended.

It can be said with full confidence that those who visualize some monetary scheme or some other government measure by which prosperity and full employment can be attained without price control do not possess a clear conception of the laws which govern our economy. Free pricing and full employment are incompatible, a fact which is well recognized by economists. During a war, perchance, when billions of dollars are added to the monetary bloodstream through government expenditures, full employment may temporarily be reached even without the implementation of price control, since prices are somewhat slow to react. Under comparative price stability, however, there is no possibility of reaching even within a reasonable proximity of full capacity utilization without price control. If we want free price competition, we must contend with market resistance, wasted capacities, and unemployment. If we want security of markets, full utilization of resources, and full employment, we must have price control. There is no other choice.

The reason for this unfortunate circumstance is, of course, that without price control the government must undertake to hold prices in check by indirect means in order to fulfill its responsibility of maintaining a sound monetary system, and the only possible way by which it can do this with each person struggling to maximize prices is to maintain a permanent insufficiency of purchasing power, a permanent difficulty of selling and finding jobs, and a permanent underutilization of productive resources. This is the price we must pay for the privilege of private pricing. Any attempt to make the purchasing power sufficient to ensure full employment, or even to reduce the deficiency, would raise prices and frustrate the effort. If we are to maintain a reasonably sound money system, we must prevent prices from spiraling out of reach; but there are only two forces which can accomplish this feat, price control and sales resistance; and if we do not have the one, we must have the other. To ask the government to remove sales resistance and marketing difficulties without applying price control would be tantamount to asking for the removal of the foundation upon which our money system is based. It would be to ask for a condition which lends itself to a galloping inflation of prices with the eventual collapse of the money system.

Since the end of the Second World War it has been the general policy of the government to counteract by monetary or fiscal means any tendency toward inflation or deflation, especially to prevent any recurrence of a catastrophe such as the Great Depression of the hungry thirties. This means that whenever there is a tendency toward increased demand and rising prices, the government must step in and apply bank credit restriction (tight money) or implement surplus financing; and whenever demand drops off and there is a tendency for prices to fall, the government will ease up on credit restriction or/and apply deficit financing, thus evening out the bumps of booms and depressions which have characterized economic behavior in the past.

Expressed in different terms, this means that the government, in an effort to keep prices in check, must endeavor to maintain a constant level of depression or economic difficulties. Whenever there appears a tendency toward prosperity or good times, the government must apply its power of suppression sufficiently punitive to check the tendency. In the opposite case it may release its pressure somewhat, but at no time must it permit prosperity and economic welfare to be realized. It must strike a blow each time the prostrate economy shows signs of rising to its feet. This is monetary price control, the most merciless and distasteful control measure that a government could be called upon to execute, being contrary to all ambitions of economic growth and welfare desirable in this day of international competition. It would be the simplest and most pleasant task for any government to place more money in the hands of the consuming public, the only possible way by which the present problem can be solved, but without price control such a move would simply bring the downfall of the money system; and to prevent this, it must keep money sufficiently scarce to inhibit price inflation, to deal out the punishment of monetary price control in sufficient doses to keep the economy permanently depressed. What else could it do?

The necessity of maintaining price stability by means of money scarcity constitutes the cause of our present dilemma and the factor which frustrates all plans and suggestions aimed at improving conditions. It would be difficult to imagine a significant improvement that did not include an increased volume of public purchasing power to absorb the products of industry; but when we consider the fact that this is the very move which the government must prevent in order to hold prices, we have a tendency to despair. A plan to spend or invest idle savings, for instance, might be considered beneficial; but if it were sufficient to improve conditions of marketing and employment, it would raise prices, and it would be necessary for the government to counter the move by heavier taxation or bank credit restriction, or both, to mop up the urgently needed purchasing power increment before it has time to cause price inflation. It is a frustrating experience of desiring to supply the people with the essential lifeblood of purchasing power but being compelled by circumstances to wrest this purchasing power away from them.

7. Volume of Unemployment

What degree of economic depression is necessary to maintain price stability? Or at what level of employment or depression will prices tend to rise or fall, requiring monetary adjustment to maintain stability? It would be hazardous, indeed, to commit oneself definitely on this question because of the many circumstances involved. Professor Joseph Aschheim of The Johns Hopkins University has estimated that five per cent unemployment is necessary for price stability (*), although neither he nor any other economist would be prepared to make a definite statement on this issue. One reason for the difficulty is that the rate of overt or registered unemployment is a very indefinite or undependable variable in which to express economic depression, being part of a greater concept of gross unemployment or gross underutilization of productive capacity. If we should use this wider concept in our calculation we might come closer to the truth, since gross unemployment is a more dependable variable. It would be possible, in fact, to vary either overt or disguised unemployment without changing total unemployment. If, for instance, the government should engage part of the unemployed in some non-essential occupation for the sake of relieving unemployment, we would have less overt unemployment but correspondingly more disguised unemployment. If, on the other hand, some type of featherbedding should be abolished, the non-essential men being laid off, we would have more unemployment and correspondingly less dis-

* Joseph Aschheim, Price-level Stability and Employment Act Objectives; The Relationship of Prices to Economic Stability and Growth; Government Printing Office, Washington, 1958.

guised unemployment, total unemployment remaining the same in both cases.

But even if we base our calculation on this wider concept of gross underutilization of capacity, we would find it difficult to estimate precisely at what unemployment level prices would remain stable under free pricing, since this level might be different in different countries and under different circumstances depending on public sentiment, social organizations, labor-management relations, industrial combines, oligopolistic or monopolistic pricing practices, or other factors which may interfere with free pricing. The best we could do is to estimate the prevailing loss of productivity in a given country and under a condition of relatively stable prices and use the figures obtained, even if these did not represent the exact loss under absolutely stable prices. If our estimate of 30 per cent gross unemployment in the present American economy is realistic, then we have the staggering fact that the stabilization of prices by monetary and fiscal means alone requires the suppression of the nation's economic activity to seventy per cent of capacity. This, then, represents the cost of monetary price control, some 150 billion dollars per year, calculated in economic values alone, let alone social, moral, ethical, and other values.

Direct government price control is the only possible means by which this tragic loss can be averted. We must have money to purchase the goods we produce, if these goods are to come to our avail, or if our productive capacity is to avail us; but we cannot have this money in sufficient quantity without price control. Private price competition causes money to dwindle, and there is nothing short of price control and credit expansion that will replenish it. No existing government, were it ever so sincere and honest, could ever supplement the deficiency of purchasing power without the benefit of price control; and no political party of whatever name or political leaning that did not include price control in its program could ever do much better.

CHAPTER V

PRICE CONTROL

1. Opinions on Price Control

Price control in itself is not a desirable objective. It necessitates government regulations, and it is a general sentiment in our free democracy that any government intervention in what the individual considers his own affair is undesirable. Government regulations are tolerated whenever proved necessary, but it is a general feeling that such regulations should be kept at a minimum, limited, that is, to what is considered absolutely necessary. The business man desires to carry on his business as free from government interference as possible. So we all do.

It is natural to expect, therefore, that a program of government price control will encounter a measure of opposition, especially in its early stages. We could not reasonably assume that each and every person concerned should realize the necessity of conferring on the government the prerogative of price determination. During the war-time emergency, 1942 to 1946, a considerable hostility toward price control was in evidence, even though it was generally conceded that this emergency measure was necessary to prevent run-away inflation of prices. Our success in creating a favorable public attitude toward price control in peacetime will depend on our success in establishing proof of its necessity or advantage in the struggle for economic and social welfare, something which can be done, perhaps, only after the measure has been brought fully into effect.

One of the obstacles to our effort in creating a more cooperative attitude toward price control is undoubtedly the still fairly general acceptance of the doctrine that price determination is a matter to be settled by mutual negotiations between buyer and seller.

The seller feels that he is selling his own merchandise and that he should be free to set the price of these goods at a rate at which he is willing to part with them. If the buyer is not willing to pay this price, he is free to turn down the deal, or he is free to offer a somewhat lower price in a bid to come to terms. According to this *laissez-faire* theory, the price will settle at a rate at which buyer and seller are both satisfied. Economists often emphasize, also, that prices are governed by the law of supply and demand and require no arbitrary control from any government source, implying, oftentimes, that the price of any commodity will settle at a rate at which supply equals demand, rise when demand exceeds supply and drop when supply exceeds demand. Government price control, according to this theory, would interfere with the law of supply and demand.

2. Wartime Attitude Toward Price Control

In the year 1942 a Committee on Price Control and Rationing was organized in the United States with the object of conducting a field study on the impact of price control on the civilian sector of American business. The object was to interview businessmen and ask questions concerning their stand in regard to price control, their actions favorable or unfavorable to price control, how price control had affected their business, etc. The interviews were conducted in the Chicago metropolitan district and nearby manufacturing towns and comprised a field of 528 firms, manufacturers, wholesalers, retailers, packers, processers, groceries, drugstores, liquor outlets, restaurants, laundries, and others.

This study, even though it covered only a limited area and a limited number of firms, is of great importance in this connection, since it gives a general idea of what we may expect in the way of opposition to or compliance with a program of price control. Some of the questions asked were: Would you say that on the whole the O. P. A. (Office of Price Administration) did a good job or a bad job, or did more good than harm, or more harm than good? What would you say were the main positive achievements of the O. P. A. in your line of business? What would you say were the main mistakes made by the O. P. A. in your line of business? Has there been an improvement or a deterioration in the administration of price control in the last few months? Are the O. P. A. orders usually clear and easy to understand? Would you say that the O. P. A. regulations were generally fair or unfair? Were some types of business benefited or hurt by the regulations? How? To what extent? Has the O.P.A. done a satisfactory job in checking up on compliance with its regulations? Would you say that the methods of enforcing price control should be changed? How? Why? What kind of formula ceiling would you appropriate? What were the effects of price control on supplies? Have price ceilings, in your opinion, hampered production? Should the O. P. A. be abolished or reorganized?

As can be expected, there was no general agreement among businessmen as to the merits or demerits of price control. Some were openly hostile while others expressed various opinions ranging to full acceptance. The committee classified respondents in two opposite groups, those who were fully cooperative and those who were hostile. Respondents who could not be classified in either of these groups were classified as intermediates.

It was found that less than one quarter of the respondents interviewed were hostile toward price control; less than one fifth was fully cooperative; while the greatest number, or 57 per cent, were placed in the intermediate group.

Many merchants in the intermediate group were strongly in favor of price control, but were critical of the O. P. A. or its practices. Some acknowledged the need for fighting inflation, but felt that individual prices should be allowed to rise. Others expressed the opinion that the O. P. A. should be more strict in its control of prices, but should not attempt "profit control." They advocated ceilings based on cost.

The committee found a marked difference of attitudes among businessmen in different industries. Thus, in the field of men's and women's wear and drugs much more favorable attitudes were revealed than in the field of meat and groceries. In men's wear, for instance, 34 per cent were fully cooperative; 6 per cent were hostile. In women's wear 21 per cent were fully cooperative;

15 per cent were hostile. In shoes and gloves 34 per cent were fully cooperative; 14 per cent were hostile. In foods, on the other hand, 13 per cent were fully cooperative and 37 per cent were hostile.

It is of interest to note, also, that more hostility was found at the beginning of the enquiry period than at a later date. Thus, in the second half of 1942, 58 per cent of the respondents in the field of meat and groceries were hostile to price control; one per cent were fully cooperative. In the first half of 1943, 42 per cent were hostile; 9 per cent were fully cooperative. In the second half of 1943, 30 per cent were hostile; 18 per cent were fully cooperative. In the field of apparel and house furnishings, the comparative figures for the three periods covered were 6%, 19%, and 8% classified as hostile and 22%, 21%, and 26% classified as fully cooperative*.

3. False Conception of the Purpose of Price Control

But whereas this survey will give some indication of what we may expect in the way of opposition to price control, it is by no means a dependable guide in peacetime. The establishment of price control as a basic constituent of a general plan of purchasing power control is an undertaking entirely different from that of a wartime emergency measure, and whether in the course of its introduction we encounter opposition or cooperation will depend on how well the people of the nation are informed of the plan, or how fully they comprehend its implication. If businessmen should learn that an immediate program of price control were to be launched with the sole intent of preventing price inflation, opposition would in all certainty be encountered, even to a greater degree than during wartime. During the war price control was tolerated partly for patriotic reasons and partly because people realized the necessity of preventing run-away inflation of prices. With no war and with no threat of rapidly rising prices, businessmen would not comprehend the need for price control. If, however, the true purpose of price control is fully understood, not as an emergency measure to stop price inflation, but as a neces-

* George Katona; *Price Control and Business;* The Principia Press, Inc., Bloomington, Indiana, (1945).

sary prerequisite to a plan of increasing and balancing purchasing power to permit full employment and full capacity production, this control measure can be expected to receive enthusiastic support. One cannot see how it could do otherwise.

Most of the adverse criticism which has been levied against peacetime price control in the past can undoubtedly be traced to a misunderstanding of its true purpose, or, shall we say, an underestimation, by pros and cons alike, of the potency of this control measure in the battle against depression and unemployment. Price control has been regarded almost exclusively as a government anti-inflation measure, with no other benefits to be derived; and with this prospect in view many businessmen have attacked the measure as a threatened restriction of profits and a dampening of business incentives. Little wonder then that the campaign for price control has met a cool reception.

It will be clear to anyone who employs deductive reasoning on this matter that the true purpose of price control is not price control as such, but an increased volume of purchasing power. In matters pertaining to this plan, we are not interested in the pricing of goods or in correcting some supposed inconsistency in this pricing. What we are interested in is the increasing and balancing of purchasing power to permit full employment. But unfortunately there is no other way of increasing purchasing power than through the medium of price control. If there were, we would not advocate price control. Price control, as we have said, is not a desirable objective in itself. Even at its best it will involve strict government supervision of price movements and the ordering of rollbacks whenever necessary to maintain stability; and before we can accede to this restraint, we must have the promise of a greater good than that of an improvement in the function of pricing, even assuming that such an improvement would be possible under government price control.

There are two divisions of pricing in which a government commission could conceivably effect an improvement, the balancing of individual prices according to supply and demand and the maintenance of the price level, but neither of these would justify the imposition of price control per se. In the division of individual pricing, for instance, there is little that the government commission could do in the way of improvement. Relative prices, as a matter of fact, are already balanced according to the law of supply and demand. Whenever a commodity shows signs of becoming scarce, private producers and dealers will promptly raise its price, and more producers will rush in to produce the commodity and supplement the scarcity. When a commodity becomes unusually abundant, its price will drop, and producers will abandon it in favor of other commodities. It would be difficult to improve on this individual price relationship, even by a well-organized control commission. In any event, relative prices are ultimately governed by the people themselves. Each person who demands to produce a commodity or who demands to consume a commodity is casting a vote which helps to determine what must be produced and what must be consumed, and thereby also what the price must be. The best that the government commission could do in this respect is to implement the price changes according to the wishes of the public, a function which is already satisfactorily performed under private control. A government commission, in fact, would have to adjust prices in much the same manner as they are now adjusted; and even assuming that there are some irregularities in present pricing practices which could be adjusted by a government price control agency, the benefits derived would definitely not be sufficient to justify the imposition of general price control.

Nor would the stabilization of the price level justify the imposition of price control, even though here we can visualize a definite improvement. The price index today is rising perhaps by three or four points per year, a rise which could undoubtedly be prevented by means of government price control; but when we consider the formidable task of introducing general price control as a means of reaching this end, we must conclude that the value gained is not worth the cost.

There is only one derivative possessing sufficient social value to justify the imposition of price control: the coefficient which makes it possible to supplement and control the nation's purchasing power. The nation that has control of prices has control of its own economic destiny. It can control and adjust purchasing power and demand to any level whatsoever, or to any level that best serves the interest of its population. No longer will it be necessary to conduct business forecasting, or to study omens ranging from sunspots to interest rates in an attempt to predict the coming of a boom, a recession, or a depression. With price control in effect, the public representative in control of the nation's credit volume will be in full control of the economic life of the nation. It could create a depression or a scarcity of goods by abusing its power of credit control, but it has also the power to adjust and balance the credit volume to the precise measure necessary to maintain production-distribution balance, a condition under which each seller can find a buyer and each buyer can find a seller. It can remove purchasing power deficiency, market bottlenecks, idle capacity, and unemployment. It can solve the problem of distribution.

It is significant to observe, however, that often when the subject of price control has come up for consideration, even those who have spoken in its favor have emphasized one or the other of the comparatively trivial benefits to be derived from the measure, and have completely missed the major issue. Thus many people campaigning in favor of price control have deplored the evils of a rising price level which deflates the value of the money unit and does injustice to pensioners or others in receipt of fixed incomes. Judging by this criterion we would assume that after price control had been brought fully into force, there would be no follow-up of any plan to increase purchasing power, to balance production and distribution, or to bring about any other improvement which would justify the imposition of price control. It implies that we would still have to contend with the same purchasing power deficiency, the same market bottleneck, and the same unemployment. All that we would benefit is the prevention of the three or four points per year rise in the price index which would otherwise be registered, a trivial matter which could largely be corrected by the escalator clause.

This proposition does not make sense, nor is it surprising if a campaign for price control should find little enthusiastic support on such a flimsy promise. A fixed price level is undoubtedly a desirable objective in an economy in which the more urgent problems of unemployment and lagging production schedules have been solved. Today, however, when industrial activity is hampered by lack of demand and the uncertainty of profits, such an objective would be of questionable value. In fact, many economists have suggested with undisputed justification that it would be better to retain a gradually rising price level than one which is absolutely fixed, since rising prices are more likely to register a profit in the books of the entrepreneur than stable prices. And, incidentally, if the stabilization of prices should be the sole issue at stake, it would be quite possible for the government to accomplish this by indirect control. All it would have to do is to clamp a further restriction on the already insufficient purchasing power, thereby creating slightly more sales resistance than we experience today—at the cost, perhaps, of a few more thousands of unemployed.

Naturally, with the implementation of price control we should establish a fixed price level. To do otherwise would be foolish, since it would hardly involve a greater task to maintain the price level fixed than to make it rise or fall or fluctuate. But what we must remember is that what makes it possible to increase and control purchasing power is not that prices are fixed, but that they are socially controlled. It would be quite possible to raise or control the nation's purchasing power even with a rising or fluctuating price level, provided that prices were under control, and not left in private hands. This fact can be ascertained by studying conditions in the Soviet Union. The Soviet Government has made no special effort to fix prices. The price level there has been as variable as in the West, if not more so. Prices, however, have been under strict government control, and for this reason it has been possible for the Government to raise the nation's purchasing power to a level far above that necessary to balance production and distribution.

It is not necessary to establish communism as a means of controlling purchasing power and conquer the problem of distribution. All we need is price and credit control. The Soviet Government has solved the problem of distribution, not because of socialism or communism, but because of price control. Price control establishes a fixed value of the monetary unit, a value which is not affected by the money volume, or by the level of demand, thus making it unnecessary to hold prices by means of money scarcity. With this assured, we can establish a balanced economy, yet retain free enterprise, private property, and individual initiative.

4. Closing the Gap Between Price and Demand

Price control and credit expansion constitute the two basic steps in our program of initiating a system of Balanced Distribution. Price control stops the multiplication of prices — except, of course, in relation to productivity; credit expansion brings consumer demand up to the price-demand level. In other words, price control stops the process by which goods are being tied from the consumer or user; credit expansion accelerates the process by which goods are being purchased or released, thus bringing the two processes into closer relation with each other.

The problem of unemployment and unsold goods and services in today's economy is caused by the inescapable actuality that the total price volume, or total figure of supply, is greater than demand. There is a limit to the amount of goods and services which consumers or buyers will purchase during a given period and under a given circumstance. Let us suppose that this amount is represented by the figure 80. But suppose that sellers during the same period request a total price of 100. Accordingly, only 80 per cent of the total price and wage demands are met. The remaining 20 per cent represents overt and disguised unemployment. Our object is to close this gap between the sellers' price and the price which buyers are willing and able to pay, a project which can be accomplished by pegging the seller's price at the figure of 100 and proceed to raise the buyer's demand from 80 to 100 by expanding the credit volume. Without price control this would not be possible, for if buyers should increase their purchases from 80 to 100 either on account of government action in expanding the money volume or on account of people's own action in circulating the money at a greater speed, sellers would quickly raise the price to 125, and the gap between the two variables would be as wide as before. And if buyers should increase their purchases to 125 on account of either of these same actions, sellers would raise their price to 150 or 160; but the gap would always be there in approximately the same value differential as before.

The explanation is, of course, that we as sellers desire the highest possible price and as buyers desire the lowest possible price, and that, being free to set our own selling price, we try for a price a little above that which we on the average are willing to pay. We often forget as sellers that we are also the buyers, and that we cannot get more for our commodities and services than we ourselves are willing to pay. We must redeem every unit of price that we place on our goods and services, if these goods and services are to come to our avail. Each by himself, however, we are trying for a price above that which is possible to realize.

There is an equilibrium price or a price-demand relationship at which all goods can be sold at full capacity, a price or price-demand relationship which permits the greatest economic welfare to all, the highest possible real income, maximum output, and maximum profits to the seller. The reason that we undertake to set the price above this level and suffer a loss is that there is no standard provided for the population to show precisely what the optimum price must be. Besides, there is no exact limit to the price which any one seller can realize, since we do not all enjoy the same sales opportunities, and we do not all exert the same efforts to sell. It will not be possible for all to sell above the equilibrium price, but it will be quite possible for some sellers to do so. Even at 80 for demand and 100 for prices, eighty per cent of the sellers could sell their full capacity, or else all sellers could sell eighty per cent of their potential output. And since it is possible for some sellers to sell at this over-the-average-maximum-obtainable price, each one will argue that he should be able to do the same. The inevitable result is that a considerable percentage of our potential product is lost in the struggle to do the impossible.

It does not mean that those who fail to sell at the competitive price are necessarily poor sellers any more than those who lose a race are necessarily poor runners. When there are more prices than the public will redeem with a given volume of money, some sellers will not be able to sell, and some workers will not be able to find employment, whether these victims are poor salesmen or not.

The rate of loss may be different in different countries and under different circumstances depending on the intensity of the price struggle between sellers and buyers. Sellers, naturally, will want the highest possible price, buyers the lowest possible price; and it is the readiness or reluctance by which the two come to terms that determines the rate of unemployment and economic loss. The more readily sellers and buyers come to terms on prices, the narrower the gap between them, and the less the rate of unemployment; and the more stubbornly sellers hold out for higher prices and buyers for lower prices, the wider the gap and the higher the rate of unemployment. If sellers should refuse to sell unless they received a given price, and if buyers at the same time should refuse to buy unless they were quoted a lower price, no sales would be made, and all men and machinery would be unemployed. It is the loss of sales resulting from the failure to agree on prices that accounts for unemployment, and the volume of unemployment could be measured in terms of the time and energy that is wasted in the futile struggle to obtain a more favorable price than is possible.

It would be a simple matter for the government through monetary or fiscal action to increase demand, let us say from 70 or 80 to 100 or whatever was necessary to meet current price claims; but it would be extremely difficult without price control to prevent prices from rising under the impact of the increased demand. If this could be done by persuasion or appeals for voluntary restraint, productivity, profits, and real incomes could be increased to a corresponding degree, and unemployment could be eliminated. The reason that it is very improbable or impossible that such an eventuality would obtain without price control is that the increased demand would remove money scarcity and sales resistance, the very factors which now keep prices from rising and upon which the present money system is based. It would create a condition under which money was plentiful and demand brisk, a condition under which goods would be purchased or taken off the market as fast as they could be produced, or under which producers and manufacturers could utilize all the mechanization and automation obtainable for maximum output and still find markets for their products, a prosperity condition reminiscent of that of wartime, with the exception that there would be no war and no wartime rationing. In short, it would create a condition under which prices would ordinarily zoom upwards in no uncertain manner; and it is very unlikely that such a condition could prevail without price control. Yet it is the condition that we must establish in order to secure full capacity production.

We might further illustrate this difficulty by an example. Suppose that the optimum or most profitable price under a given circumstance is represented by the figure 80, and also that businessmen enjoy generally the same opportunity to sell, or exert generally the same sales pressure. If under these circumstances a firm should set its price at, let us say, 40, its returns would obviously dwindle. Even though it would receive a tremendous demand for its commodities for as long as these lasted, it would be operating at a loss, and would be forced out of business. But suppose now that it should proceed to raise its price by a gradual progression to 50, 60, 70, 80, 90, 100, and so forth. Obviously its returns, or profits would gradually increase until it had reached the figure of 80, after which these returns or profits would again dwindle by a gradual process until the firm had been forced out of business by the lack of profits. But the difficulty consists in the fact that being free to set its own price each firm, company and corporation is endeavoring to set a price above the optimum level in an attempt to realize additional profit, with the result that profits decline. Today we maintain a price of, for instance, 100, and the profits, or returns, are down to 70 per cent of capacity. And, naturally, since the majority of salesmen are attempting to realize a price above the realizable level, it would be futile for any one firm to lower its price to what would otherwise be the most profitable level, since it is dependent upon purchasing its supplies from other firms at the inflated price. If it should attempt to do so, it would again be operating at a loss. This means that the general struggle that now is in vogue to set a price which lowers business returns compels each and every businessman to follow suit. He has no other choice.

It is often said that businessmen are seeking to maximize profits, and are directing their pricing policy toward this objective. But this is true only in so far as it concerns the action of the individual firm. It is not true when businessmen in general are considered. The fact is, on the contrary, that businessmen in general are exerting their best efforts to suppress their own profits, and the only way to prevent them from doing so is to compel them through the medium of price control to maintain a price level which permits a sufficient volume of purchasing power to absorb the products of industry. Freedom to vie for the maximum of profits through price competition will suppress profits to a percentage of what they might be through a healthier competition for output and sales under price control.

This does not mean to say that we should undertake to force down prices to a level at which they would meet current demand occasioned by today's credit volume. To do so would entail an unwarranted shifting of property from debtor to creditor. The debtor would have to repay his debt in a "bigger" dollar, a high price to pay for the sole purpose of changing the size of the measuring unit. The object is, of course, to retain the price level as is and proceed to increase the volume of credit.

5. Demand Control

Some economists have expressed opposition to price control on the ground that it would create scarcity of goods and necessitate rationing. Their argument is that under free competition supply and demand will generally balance, or will automatically adjust themselves to restore balance. When there is more money chasing goods than there are goods to buy, prices will rise; and when goods are in excess of the money available to buy them, prices will drop. When supply equals demand, prices will stabilize. If prices are prevented from rising at a time when demand is in excess of supply (such as during wartime), scarcity will appear, and rationing becomes necessary. The excess purchasing power must then be accumulated as savings.

This argument, incidentally, is correct, considering that what the economist means by supply is the commodities actually available for sale. As we have already pointed out, the supply of goods actually produced and available for sale may fairly well balance with demand under any economic conditions, even under a severe depression, the reason being that the businessman will not usually order or produce goods much in excess of what he can expect to sell within a reasonable time. Prices, in fact, are not governed by the relationship between demand and total supply but by the relationship between demand and net supply of actually available commodities. The soldiers who lie dead on the battlefield do no longer decide the outcome of the battle. This outcome is determined by those who are still fighting. Similarly, prices are not determined by the millions of unemployed — who, in fact, have lost their franchise of price determination — but by those who are still in business; and if there should be an increase in demand or an easing of sales resistance, prices would rise irrespective of unemployment. This explains the phenomenon that in 1932, when perhaps more than half of our productive capacity lay idle, prices began to rise. According to the supply-demand theorem, we would explain this by saying that at that time demand was in excess of supply, even though this would seem ludicrous when potential supply is considered.

It is true, also, that scarcity of marketed goods could become a reality at any stage of the business cycle, if demand was brought in excess of available supplies. At the start of World War Two, for instance, when rationing had to be introduced in the United States because of scarcity, the nation still had some six million unemployed. This same experience could quite likely become a reality if today we should apply price ceilings and proceed to increase the credit volume. The reason is, of course, that whereas there is a huge potential supply in the form of unemployed men, machinery, and resources, this supply is not yet ready to meet the increased consumer demand. To place these goods on the market ready for the consumer requires time, especially if workers are to be employed under the most advanced mechanical conditions. It requires plant, machinery, raw materials, and the necessary development process; and if purchasing power should be expanded too rapidly, scarcity of goods might become a disappointing experience.

What the economist in this case fails to emphasize, however, is that scarcity of goods, whenever such is the eventuality, is caused by credit control, not by price control. Price control per se cannot cause scarcity, nor can it increase demand. During the war, admittedly, when the credit volume was brought to extreme proportion through war financing, price control aggravated the situation by helping to maintain the purchasing power of the dollar. Generally speaking, however, price control cannot cause inflation any more than a yardstick can build a skyscraper. Price control establishes a standard for the measurement of economic values, nothing more and nothing less. Distribution is governed by credit control. Thus, if at any time during the development of Balanced Distribution there should be a scarcity of marketed goods, the fault would not lie with the commission in control of prices, but with the commission in control of credit. The idea is, of course, to bring purchasing power to a point at which markets, economic growth, and the progress toward full employment and full capacity production are assured, yet a point at which no shortages of marketed goods will manifest themselves, this purchasing power level to be maintained permanently by immaculate government control of prices and credit.

The pessimist might impart, for instance, that we must have either unemployment or scarcity, or both, or that if purchasing power is brought to a point which permits economic expansion, it will also bring scarcity. But this opinion undoubtedly stems from the observation of human behavior under an insecure economy, an economy under which neither prices nor supplies can be depended on. Human action will be considerably different under a secure and balanced economy than under one which is uncontrolled and uncertain. Bank panics, buying sprees, hoarding, money hoarding, booms and depressions, and any such vicissitudes as have been our experience in the past can undoubtedly be traced to uncertainties of the conditions upon which some economic good depends. A fear that prices will drop, for instance, will cause people to think that now is the time to accumulate savings and to sell out stocks on hand before prices go lower. The result is economic stagnation. A fear of scarcity or rising prices, on the other hand, will cause people to think that the right time has come to spend money and to accumulate inventories and personal supplies. The result of this action is rising prices and scarcity. In an economy in which price maintenance as well as supply maintenance is absolutely assured by responsible government control, such panic action will not occur. There will be no need for the dealer, for instance, to accumulate undue inventories for fear of scarcity, or even to desist from such accumulation for fear of lower prices. Nor will there be any cause for fear to invest money in capital or to prepare long-term industrial planning on suspicion of the lack of markets. Naturally there will be some unavoidable uncertainties, especially in regard to obsolescence, but there could be nothing comparable to those of today. If the purchasing power is correctly balanced and maintained at the optimum level, the progress toward full employment and maximum production will in all certainty take its normal course.

6. The Laissez-Faire Theory

During the laissez-faire era of the nineteenth and early twentieth centuries it was widely believed that if people were left free of any government interference and the law of supply and demand were allowed free play, the maximum of economic welfare for all would be assured. Supply and demand would always tend to balance at full employment and full capacity. If demand should increase and threaten scarcity and labor shortage, prices would rise and restore equilibrium. If demand should drop off and cause surplus stocks and unemployment, prices would drop and restore full employment. An increased demand would raise prices only if full employment and full capacity production prevailed. If some unemployment existed, an increased demand would not cause prices to rise until full employment had been reached.

Of recent decades this theory has received a serious blow. It has become more and more clear to economists and government advisors that the government of today must fight unemployment and rising prices at the same time. Prices, in fact, have risen almost continuously since the bottom of the depression in 1932, and are still rising despite millions of unemployed and a huge productive potential lying dormant because of the lack of demand. Those who still lean toward the laissez-faire theory put blame for our troubles on "administered prices," that is, prices that are set by large labor unions and large industrial corporations and combines. The argument is that the individual is no longer free to set his own price in the market, that this price is often set for him by oligopolies, and that prices on this account are forced above those governed by supply and demand, causing unsold goods and unemployment. It implies, in other words, that administered prices tend to be higher relative to demand than they would be if the individual himself was permitted to decide.

There are at least two serious objections to this theory. In the first place, there is no proof that the theory holds true, or that there would be any easing of the price struggle if small business units and small labor groups were to decide prices. All that we know is that purely competitive prices respond more readily to changes in demand than do administered prices. Administered prices are more stable, dropping slower with a drop in demand and rising slower with an increase in demand; but there is no proof that on the whole these prices are forced higher. This may be so in the case of the price of labor, since unionized labor has more power to press wage claims. In the case of merchandise sold by large chain stores or products sold by large industrial concerns, there is grave doubt. Empirically we would assume that the opposite is true, that small business units will tend to demand higher prices than their larger counterparts.

But even if the theory should prove to be true, we cannot see what kind of solution would be appropriate, or what kind of actions would be effective in dealing with the problem. Would this consist in breaking up labor unions and large business concerns and dividing industry into small handicrafts? It seems reasonable to conclude that such a move would be a step backward, a process of going back a century or two in time, yet with no assurance that the problem would find its solution. It appears more logical, on the contrary, that we should endeavor to establish more unity both within labor and within industry, for upon such unity we must depend in future years for a rational approach to price and wage determination. Labor unions, chain stores and other large business units constitute, in fact, an appreciable beginning of the unity we need for the maintenance of price stability and purchasing power.

7. The Need for Understanding and Cooperation

If the public should fully appreciate the purpose of price control and conduct themselves accordingly, our task would be greatly simplified. In fact, it would be unnecessary to enforce strict price regulation, if businessmen or salesmen in general should decide to cooperate voluntarily in maintaining price stability despite an increased demand. All that the government would have to do in this case is to assume the responsibility of credit control, to gradually increase the credit volume to a point at which full capacity production was assured and to maintain it in this position. The problem which we must face is that each of the millions who now control prices thinks that he will benefit from an increased price, and that it would be extremely difficult to convince him that this is not so. The best we could do, perhaps, is to prove that an increase in his price will not benefit him if all others raise their price to the same degree. But we still have the problem of assuring him that if he refrains from raising his price, all others will do the same. If this can be assured, he might consider the idea of price restraint.

A price control or price limitation campaign to increase purchasing power, however, has a disadvantage in that it appears to be against the interest of the individual businessman. A campaign to raise prices might receive more enthusiastic support, since in the opinion of many businessmen the thing to do to increase purchasing power is to raise prices. The irony of the situation is, of course, that the solution of the present problem lies in doing what seems to be the opposite of our personal good; and it is for this reason that the problem has defied centuries of effort. We are struggling in the wrong direction. A rabbit caught in a snare will keep pulling in one direction in an effort to release himself, while the snare squeezes tighter and tighter around his neck. A slight move in the opposite direction would release the snare and allow him by means of simple motion to slip the wire over his neck and escape. But to him there is only one logical way to solve his problem, viz., to pull away from the snare that is holding him, and he perishes in the struggle. Similarly it would be easy for us to solve the present problem of purchasing power deficiency and unemployment by doing the opposite to what we individually think will benefit us, to lower prices or, better yet, to refrain from raising prices while the money volume was increased. Yet we exert all efforts to do the opposite, and every one of our efforts to raise incomes by raising prices above the level of demand will result in a loss of income to the same measured extent. And if we continue the struggle, we will eventually suffer the same fate as the rabbit.

It would be a futile endeavor, however, to persuade the public to voluntary refrain from raising prices under the impact of purchasing power sufficiency, as long as each individual by himself will benefit from a rise in his prices. Undoubtedly a strong public appeal to hold the price line would do some good. A great many businessmen, in fact, might comply with the appeal, permitting some increase in purchasing power without a corresponding increase in prices. It could not possibly be a success, however, since there are always those who take a more or less hostile attitude toward society and would grab any chance to take advantage of the experiment. The best that we could expect is a partial or temporary success. And the sad part of the situation is that the loyal persons who complied with the appeal would suffer a loss to the benefit of those who did not comply. A half-way measure, therefore, would be worse than nothing. It would be unfair and unjust. It would be to ask the loyal persons to make a sacrifice to the benefit of the recalcitrants. Price control will administer justice only if it applies equally to all.

But in order that we may have price limitation obligations extended to all we must have the social organization necessary to carry out this complex task. In other words, we must have a competent and responsible price control commission. A price control commission may appear different to different people depending on their point of view or upon their standing in regard to price control. However, if we recognize the fact that price control obligations must be extended to all in order that we may enjoy the benefit of full purchasing power, we must consider a price control commission as a necessary medium through which this economic objective can be reached. Logically, we should look upon a price control commission as a common organization in which we are all members and through which our interests in the common cause of purchasing power sufficiency are being served.

The plain fact is, however, that before we can hope to realize the aims and objects of price control and credit expansion there must be an improved public understanding of this reform program and a more conciliatory attitude toward it. We cannot launch a program of this size without a clear view of what we wish to do. The most important prerequisite in any human undertaking is a purpose. Undoubtedly a great many people today would welcome a program of price control, housewives, wage earners, pensioners, since such a program would stop creeping inflation which deflates the value of the money unit; but it is not good enough to institute price control without the main object in view. Businessmen, who by all logical calculation should be the greatest beneficiaries, have smeared the program with a varying degree of reproach. Some businessmen have denounced peacetime price control as a government measure to control profits and meddle in private affairs, and have contended that the measure would destroy business incentives and cause economic stagnation, that it would mean the end of free enterprise and a step toward dictatorship, that it would cause stock markets to crash and business to slump, that it would necessitate government control of production and lead to communism, that it would suppress prices and profits which provide the necessary motive for business enterprise and cause widespread unemployment. The argument is that businessmen want high prices; for when prices are high, profits are good, and business activity is brisk. Price control would create a low-price economy.

This kind of argument serves to prove that the critics, whether pro or con, completely ignore the principal and, in fact, the only justifiable cause for price control, viz., an increased volume of purchasing power, and consider price control merely as a measure to control prices, taking for granted that the problem of distribution and unemployment is inevitable, whether we have price control or not. It explains also the lack of appreciation which has been shown President Kennedy's efforts to check price increases and reduce taxes. If the true purpose of price control is fully understood, it is inconceivable that the businessman could find reasonable cause for complaint. The contention that price control would restrict profits and dampen business motives would not in this case appear sensible. It is explicit from all angles of reasoning that the very opposite is true. This can be ascertained by considering the basic steps which must be taken in the course of initiating a program of purchasing power expansion and balanced distribution. These steps, as we have said, include the pegging of prices at the prevailing level and proceed gradually to expand credit by means of reduced taxation or otherwise to a level at which buying and selling demands are balanced. What could possibly have happened at this stage which could not be classified as beneficial to profits and business motives? The price level has not changed; it remains at the same point as before the inception of the project. Nor have individual prices changed relative to what they would have been without price control. The price of individual items must in any case be governed by the law of supply and demand and could not be greatly different whether we have price control or not. The only significant change that has taken place is that the money or purchasing power in the hands of the public has increased and is now sufficient to purchase and absorb all that can be produced at full capacity and full employment. The economy has changed from a comparatively depressed condition to a condition of prosperity reminiscent of that of wartime. It should now be possible for businessmen to realize considerably more profits than before the plan was introduced.

If there is any doubt about this possibility, let us assume that we reverse the process and go back to the situation prevailing before the commencement of the experiment. To do so in the most orderly manner we would retain price control until the reconversion was complete. In the meantime we would proceed to withdraw credit by extra heavy taxation, bank credit restriction, or otherwise until the purchasing power of the nation had been brought down to the level necessary for monetary price control.

At the beginning of this credit-withdrawal program some sales resistance would be noticed, resulting in a measure of disguised unemployment. As we continued the program, this resistance would increase, and all the symptoms of a low purchasing power economy would reappear: stocked-up inventories, super-sales pressure, close-down of plants and factories, bankruptcies, unemployment. As soon as we felt that sales conditions were sufficiently difficult to hold prices without direct control, we would remove price ceilings, and the reversal program would be complete. At this point the price level as well as individual price relations would still be the same as originally. The only difference in this case is that the purchasing power of the nation has again been reduced to the level at which it stood before the commencement of the experiment, and we are back where we started. It is plain from all cogent reasonings that the businessman is now in a poorer position to carry on business with any assurance of profit. The economy has reverted from a condition of prosperity to that of — in comparative terms — a depression.

8. Prices versus Credit

It is a most common observation in our environment that the individual (company, corporation) desires the highest possible price for his commodities or services. The fisherman wants the highest possible price for his fish; the farmer wants the highest possible price for his corn and his potatoes; the working man wants the highest possible price for his labor; the dealer wants the highest possible price for his merchandise. Yet it is not the price that anyone wants, but the money or credit which he can get in exchange for his price. Prices do not enrich us, nor do they contribute to our possessions. The element which contributes to our economic welfare is the credit, provided that it is backed by a balanced volume of goods and services. The reason that we endeavor our best to create price, the element that ties goods in the market, is that this is the manner in which we in free enterprise economy must come into possession of credit. And the higher we can push our prices and still sell our specialities, the more money we make.

No person, however, could receive money or credit in exchange for his prices unless someone was willing to purchase his speciality, nor could we collectively receive more credit in exchange for our prices than people as consumers and users were willing to negotiate. The total purchasing demand sets the limit to the amount of credit or income we can realize through the process of pricing. And the fate or irony is, as we have already indicated, that every unit of price above this limit results in a loss of income to the same measured extent. If the total purchasing demand should be fixed at the figure of 100 and we should set our total (full capacity) price also at 100, our total potential output of goods and services would be purchased, and we would have full capacity production and full employment. If, however, we should set our total price at 110, our real income would be reduced by about ten per cent. Our gross potential product would then be divided into 110 units instead of the original 100; and since we cannot or will not purchase more than 100 units, the extra ten units will constitute a loss in the form of unemployment or unused capacity. If we should set our total price at 200 under the same circumstances, our real income would be down to 50 per cent of the original. Total capacity in this case would be divided into 200 units, and our goods-releasing power is sufficient for only 100 units. If we should set our total price at 1000, our real income would be down to ten per cent of capacity. Ninety per cent of the total price in this case would be unquoted or implied in the form of gross unemployment, human and material. If, on the other hand, we should set our total price at 90 or at any figure under 100, we would have surplus purchasing power which we could not use.

The reason that today we are exerting our best effort to push the total price above the level of demand and suffer a loss is, of course, that goods in our free enterprise economy are sold by individuals and private parties each of whom benefits individually from an increased price. In a communist country where everything was sold by the state, no one would want higher prices. On the contrary, each person would be clamoring for lower prices while at the same time appealing for higher wages and salaries. It is for this reason that as soon as communism is established in a country, goods seem to disappear, and purchasing power becomes abundant. In our society there is a consistent urge to force prices above our power to release them with the result that we are tying goods out of our own reach. Neither communism nor capitalism has as yet learnt to establish the fundamental economic principle of balancing prices and credit.

Since each person, broadly speaking, must obtain his income through the medium of price, there is a confusion in the public mind as to what is preferable, high prices or low prices, or a high-price economy or a low-price economy. Some people contend that high prices will provide more income. The workingman will argue that if he receives higher wages, he will have more purchasing power and will be able to buy more goods. The producer, the manufacturer and dealer, likewise, will argue that if they receive higher prices they will have more spending power and will help to boost demand and stimulate business activity. Hence, they contend, high prices are preferable. And to prove their point, they might call attention to the fact that during the war when prices were high, the businessman made profits, and the economy was booming, whereas during the depression when prices were low, conditions were desperate.

A moment's reflection will convince us that it is the availability of credit or purchasing power that stimulates business activity, not prices. Rising prices is the result of an increased demand, not the cause of this demand. Government financing during the war increased purchasing power and demand to such an extent that businessmen were able to raise prices and still sell their commodities. The reason that they made good profits was not that prices were high, but that money was plentiful and people were ready to purchase the goods despite the increased price. If prices were raised at a time when demand were insufficient to negotiate this raise, profits and incomes would slump.

"High prices" has no meaning in itself. In order to carry sense, the expression must make clear in what relationship prices are high. But there are only two such relationships, that is to say, prices may be high in comparison with those of some other time in the past, or they may be high in comparison with the money available to redeem them; but neither of these relationships will indicate a preference for high prices. That prices are higher than at some other time in the past could mean only that the money unit has a lower value, but this could have no more significance than that of a change to a different standard, such as the frank, the mark, the peso, or the pound sterling. We cannot see how this could have anything to do with economic conditions. In fact, prices during a prosperity or a recession today may be twice as high as they were during a corresponding prosperity or recession a few decades ago. On the other hand, high prices relative to the supply of money available is obviously a disadvantage and, in fact, the very cause of our problem. Admittedly, profits are good and business and employment are flourishing when prices are rising, but this is not because prices are rising but because purchasing power and demand is rising so as to make it possible for businessmen to sell more goods and employ more labor. Rising prices is not necessary for improved business activity and increased incomes, but what is necessary is that demand conditions should be such that prices under unrestrained pricing would rise but are prevented from doing so through price control. This condition represents what we may call a "mildly repressed inflation."

9. The Contrast of Price Control Objectives

Price control has been resorted to on a number of occasions in the past, but the cause for which it has been implemented is in some respects the very opposite to that with which we are concerned here. This fact can be ascertained by observing the time schedules which former price control advocates have found the most appropriate for the implementation of this control measure. Accepting price control as a preliminary step toward an increased volume of purchasing power, we would conclude that the most appropriate time to implement price control is during a depression or recession when public purchasing power is insufficient to absorb potential output and men are unemployed, and the more depressed the condition the more urgent it is to implement price control. The times selected for this control measure in the past, however, have been periods of prosperity or industrial boom when purchasing power or demand has already been sufficient or more than sufficient to absorb current output, and when the promise of full employment was near at hand. These times were ostensibly the two world wars, when emergency war financing brought purchasing power and demand to excess proportions, and again in 1951, when, due to the Korean war, panic buying and scarcity of goods were anticipated, something which, incidentally, did not materialize. This serves to prove that these price control programs were initiated without any concern whatsoever for the problems of depression and unemployment. Looked upon from the standpoint of the distributive problem, they were initiated at times when this control measure was the least essential, times when demand was sufficient to bring nationwide prosperity, and unemployed men and women were being absorbed in industry, which had sprung into new life.

We do not hereby mean to say that price control during the war was unnecessary or unwise. What we mean is that price control during the war was initiated for a very different reason than that of solving the problem of distribution. It was designed to combat inflation, not to overcome a depression; to counteract the effects of an excess of purchasing power, not to supplement the deficiency of this purchasing power. Both control measures, undoubtedly, are important. However, looked upon from a sociological point of view, we must conclude that a depression is a far greater evil and a far greater justification for the imposition of price control than rising prices.

The reason why the nation during past instances has undertaken the formidable task of enforcing general price control to prevent rising prices but has not lifted a finger in the same direction to cure the demoralizing curse of unemployment can be attributed only to a failure by governments and by the public at large to properly diagnose our economic problem. There is not a more convincing proof of this failure than the helpless indecision and inaction with which the Great Depression in the early thirties was encountered. We endured then a condition which could quite easily have been overcome by a program of purchasing power expansion, a program which could have been accomplished by means of a general price-freeze and a drastic reduction — if not a complete cessation — of taxation. As we know, nothing to this effect was done until after the outbreak of the war when, happily, most of the agony of the depression had come to an end, and the nation was on its way to recovery. Then, at last, price control was initiated to accomplish the comparatively trivial task of preventing prices from rising at a faster rate than usual.

Today, again, we have a superabundance of supply in the form of overt and disguised unemployment waiting for an increase in demand, millions of men and women enduring the reproach of enforced idleness and charity, human wastage which could be turned into oceans of wealth and enrich each and all, were it not for the lack of purchasing power. Yet we stand helpless before the task, not knowing what to do.

CHAPTER VI

PRICE CONTROL METHODS

1. Comparative Levels of Purchasing Power under Price Control

The task of controlling prices is neither easy nor pleasant. It is a duty which we would rather dispense with if there were some other way of solving the problem at hand. The person who is about to undergo an operation would much rather consent to some other formula for dealing with his troubles, perhaps a few pills or some other oral medicine. So, also, we would much rather solve the problem of purchasing power deficiency by printing more paper notes or, simpler yet, by reducing taxes. Unfortunately, there is no easy way of solving the present problem. If there had been, we would have had full employment already. The best that we can do today is to face the problem of price control openly and squarely, whether it constitutes a pleasant duty or not.

It must not be assumed, however, that the control of prices will necessarily be an unpleasant chore, or that it will necesarily be a repetition of the wartime performance of this control measure. There are strong reasons to believe that price control in the peacetime economy will meet with considerably less grief than that during wartime. This can be ascertained by deductive deliberations on the relative circumstances involved. The wartime price control authorities, in the first place, had to contend with a level of purchasing power much higher than that which the peacetime economy calls for; and it will be understood that the higher the level of purchasing power the more difficult it will be to hold prices, and the more grief this function will generate. A coil spring will increase its power of resilience the farther it is extended. In its natural position it will retain a fixed length without the exertion of any physical force; but as soon as it is extended beyond this length, a force is required to maintain the increased length; and the farther it is extended, the greater force is required to keep it in its extended position. Similarly, it would not be necessary for the government to prescribe any particular price restraint if the level of purchasing power were kept sufficiently low to hold prices without price control. It is only as we raise the purchasing power above the competitive level by monetary or fiscal means that government price control measures become necessary; and the higher we raise public buying power, the greater the inflationary pressure, and the more difficult it will be to prevent prices from spiralling out of reach. A slight increase in purchasing power above the level required to hold prices without price control, a condition such as that which we experience today, would cause only a weak tendency for prices to rise, and would require only a moderate restraining force to counteract. Perhaps an appeal for voluntary restraint would be sufficient. If, however, we want to raise the purchasing power sufficiently to ensure a healthy progress toward full employment and a balanced distribution, we must expect a fairly strong upward pressure on prices; and we could not escape the chore of restraining price inflation through government-imposed price control.

The difficulty and unpleasantness of controlling prices, however, become particularly evident, not when the purchasing power is balanced, but when it is excessive and shortages of marketed goods appear, for at this point all the evils of panic buying, hoarding, rationing, blackmarketing, and price ceiling evasions become the order of the day. When there is more money in circulation than there are goods to buy, people will compete to purchase scarce commodities, and will bid a great deal more than the ceiling price in an effort to obtain the desirable items. Businessmen will hide commodities under the counter for selected customers, who are willing to pay double the price. Under these conditions, price control becomes a distasteful chore. It becomes unpleasant, not only because it is difficult to enforce, but also because it appears unjustified and foolish. It causes resentment and hostility and disrespect for government regulations. What is wrong, of course, is not price control but credit control. If the credit control commission, as we must assume, performs its solemn duty of balancing the nations credit to the exact volume necessary to absorb the goods produced without causing scarcity, price control will not be an unpleasant duty. Even admitting that it will involve checking an inflationary pressure by direct control, it will not entail the grief and antagonism with which wartime price control authorities had to contend. There will be no shortages of goods, no rationing, no blackmarketing; and the temptation to evade price ceilings will be greatly reduced.

2. Flexibility of Individual Prices

The second reason for believing that price control established as a permanent feature in the peacetime economy will entail fewer disagreeable circumstances than those of wartime is that the commission delegated with the task of bringing the program into realization will find occasion for a more thoroughgoing preparation and planning to ensure that the system will operate satisfactorily, especially in regard to the adjustment of individual prices according to supply and demand. The method of price control used during the war was, as we know, to promulgate a general price and wage freeze to be effective immediately, with the provision that no person who was in the business of selling was permitted to raise prices above the existing rate. It will be understood that such a plan would not be satisfactory as a permanent establishment in the peacetime economy, since individual prices must, in any case, remain flexible to allow for changes in supply and demand. Some commodities may become especially popular, and their price must be raised so as to encourage production and prevent shortages; while other commodities may become obsolete or lose their popularity, and their price must be reduced to prevent overproduction. Again, the production of some commodities may become greatly facilitated by new working methods, new inventions, or new resources; and the price of these commodities must be reduced to discourage production or encourage consumption; while the production of others may become more laborious through the exhaustion of natural resources or otherwise; and the price of these commodities must be increased to prevent shortages. A general price freeze may be adequate for a very limited period; but it seems logical that the longer it is in effect, the more out of proportion the individual prices are likely to be, and the more complaints and adverse criticism the price control authorities will be exposed to.

The conditions existing at the beginning of hostilities, however, called for immediate action. When, for instance, the GMPR (General Maximum Price Regulations) were issued in the United States in April 1942 the nation was experiencing rapidly rising prices, and it was felt that something drastic had to be done without delay to put a halt to the depreciation of the dollar. There was no time to plan for individual price adjustments, since, in any case, the war was not expected to last long. The sole object of the measure was to meet the temporary emergency of the war.

Obviously an emergency condition of this kind does not exist today, and it would seem inappropriate to take such a drastic step as to enforce a general price and wage freeze. Our object is not to meet a temporary emergency but to establish price control as a permanent institution in the peacetime economy, looking forward for decades, perhaps centuries; and our immediate concern must be to prepare a well-organized plan which will ensure satisfactory performance in perpetuity, not only with regard to the maintenance of a constant price level, but also with regard to the adjustment of individual prices in accordance with the law of supply and demand. And even though, admittedly, this will not be an easy task, we have at least the advantage of the element of time for planning; and if the project is approached with wisdom and determination, there is no reason why a satisfactory performance of price control cannot be introduced and perpetuated.

3. Direct and Indirect Pricing

A third and most important reason for taking an optimistic viewpoint of price control performance in the peacetime economy is the possibility that businessmen and the public in general will realize the benefit of maintaining price stability under increased demand and will co-operate with authorities in fulfilling this program. This possibility is of supreme importance, for upon it depends to a large extent whether price control will be easy or difficult, agreeable or disagreeable. If businessmen should fully appreciate the necessity of maintaining price stability to permit an increased purchasing power and should themselves take concerted action in fulfilling this objective, the government's task in controlling prices would be simple, indeed. In fact, it would be possible under such conditions to maintain price stability and full employment without much if any direct government control of prices. This function could be conferred on a business association operated by businessmen in the interest of their common good.

Nor is it visionary or utopian to speculate on such a possibility, considering that reason must in any case win out in the end. The reasonable businessman knows that if price stability can be maintained, purchasing power and demand can be increased for the good of all; and he would do anything in his power to assist the implementation and maintenance of such an arrangement, not only for his own good, but also for the good of the nation and for the security of free democracy. But by himself he could do nothing. As long as the majority of businessmen continue unreservedly their struggle to maximize prices, nothing that he could do would be of any avail. If he should attempt to hold his prices while credit restriction was eased sufficiently to relieve sales resistance, all that would happen is that his profits would be squeezed out of existence, and he would be forced out of business. But if through the medium of a common association he could exert pressure on the main body of businessmen to hold the price line, he would be happy, not only to hold his own prices, but also to take an active part in the operation of the association and to assist in maintaining the rules and regulations with which each member had to comply; and price administration, or price restraint could be a voluntary activity of businessmen instead of an arbitrary enactment of the government. What the government would have to do is to take the initial step of uniting all persons in the business of selling into a common organization in which each member was obligated by oath and allegiance to maintain a level of prices prescribed in his particular line.

We must not take for granted, however, that such an arrangement will be possible, or that the necessary co-operation for its execution will be forthcoming. Overoptimism could lead to serious disappointment. If we are to realize price stability under full employment, the government must be prepared to take such steps as will be adequate in fulfilling the objective, even if this implies direct control. Price control may assume a variation of government-business relationships, depending on public response, economic success, social organization or otherwise; and it would be difficult to conjecture what form it will take at any given time. It may have to be different, more direct and more compulsory in the beginning than at a later stage, a matter which must be decided as time goes by and more experience is gained. Generally price control is visualized as a system by which the government determine at what price goods must be sold and stipulates when this price must be raised or lowered; and even though we do not expect that this direct method of pricing will be necessary as a general rule, it is safe to say that the government commission must assume the responsibility of direct control, whenever such is necessary.

Under ordinary circumstances it will seem unnecessary for the government to directly engage in the business of pricing, just as it will seem unnecessary for the same government to directly build a bridge or erect a building. The bridge or the building can be let out to a contractor who will take full responsibility for the construction. The same is true in respect to pricing. It will be quite permissible for the businessman, especially a dealer who handles a large variety of merchandise, to raise or lower the price of the individual items he sells without any special consent from the commission. But it is obvious that before he can have the privilege of doing so under price control he must give the assurance that he will assume the responsibility of maintaining the level of prices that is appropriate within his particular field. Generally he could not raise the price of some commodities without lowering the price of others to the same extent, unless he happens to be dealing in a line whose commodities needed a price increase to comply with supply-demand requirements. This means that he would be free to raise and lower prices in compliance with the law of supply and demand, but he could not raise prices in defiance of price stability, or the standard of value. Generally he would have to retain a fixed price level; and if he were in a line whose supply and demand conditions called for a reduction in price, he would have to reduce his level of prices.

To directly fix the price of goods in the process of control would seem unnecessary in many cases. Let us consider, for example, the case of a large, nationwide chain store. This store has a competent management and staff, experienced in the process of pricing. It knows when the price of some commodities must be reduced on account of spoilage, obsolescence, or otherwise. It knows also when commodities have a tendency to become scarce and production must be encouraged by an increased price. It would seem unnecessary for the government commission to directly engage in the pricing of goods in this store. But what is absolutely necessary is that an agreement be reached between the commission and the store whereby the management of the store accepts the responsibility of price maintenance which otherwise would lie with the commission. There must be some person or persons attached to the store who become responsible to the government for the maintenance of prices. The store must also accede to government inspection, or to the admission of government officials on the duty of compiling price indexes. It may also be called upon to have prices clearly marked on each article sold, or have price listings readily available. The same regulations may apply to all mercantile or business units.

To execute price control by means of stipulating the price at which specific commodities must be sold at a given time may be quite satisfactory in the case of certain well standardized commodities, especially those that are included in the general consumer price index, since these number only a few hundred. To control all prices by this method, however, would constitute a nebulous task, considering that the number of commodity variations count up to the millions and that each of these commodities may have to be priced differently in different stores and in different cities, towns and areas of the country, as well as through their various stages of production. Certainly, the indirect or representative method by which the dealer or seller administers his own prices under the solemn promise of price restraint, will be preferable in most cases. It may not be as specific in its regulations as is the direct pricing method, but it certainly is simpler, more agreeable, and less dictatorial. It relieves the commission of a great deal of tedious work and study in order to determine what the price of each individual commodity must be at any given time. It also carries with it the promise of a system under which the selling public will ultimately retain price stability under full employment without much government interference.

In its early stages price control will undoubtedly be found a momentous undertaking under either method; for whereas there are millions of commodities to price in the one case, there are millions of business units to deal with in the other. And even though there are means by which price control can be facilitated, such as the standardization of commodities and the unification of many small business units into larger corporations or associations, there still remains the problem of removing initial suspicion and prejudice and of creating the public confidence that is necessary for an effective and harmonious execution of price control.

4. Considerations on Wage Control

At this time we might ask: Is it necessary to control the price of labor (wages) along with all other prices? In answer to this question we might say that wage control is not in itself a part of our general program of increasing and maintaining purchasing power and is not necessary to this program. The purpose of price control, as we have pointed out, is that of anchoring prices so as to make possible an increased volume of purchasing power through credit expansion. And the prices which we are particularly concerned with in this program are, of course, commodity prices, especially retail or consumer prices, which constitute the principal factor in the determination of money values. The price of the labor employed by a corporation is not an important factor in this evaluation, considering that the commodities produced by the corporation are already subject under price control, wages being a part of the cost of production. The determination of wage rates concerns the divisioning of the corporate income between management and labor, apparently a domestic issue which should be settled between the two parties involved. If wages were placed under government control, it would be for reasons other than those of maintaining national purchasing power. It would be for the purpose of settling the question concerning what part of the product, or the national income, belongs to labor and what part belongs to management or other interests.

Wages, however, may have to be subject to control for one important reason: to protect the indispensable element of profit. Today this is accomplished by means of raising prices. It is common knowledge in our environment that when labor launches a campaign for higher wages, through strike action or otherwise, management will grant the increase and then proceed to raise the price of their products in an effort to retain a margin of profit. This is what the economist calls cost-push inflation, a practice which helps to create unemployment. Under price control this method of meeting wage demands could not be done, unless, perhaps, if the commodities produced were in short demand and required an increase in price to comply with supply-demand regulations. Generally, however, the price could not be raised, which means that wage demands could reasonably be met only in relation to productivity. If despite this fact labor should press for wage increases not warranted by current productivity gains, profits might be squeezed out of existence, and the employer forced out of business. This would create unemployment despite the sufficiency of purchasing power and demand. It would create a condition under which the employer could quite readily find markets for everything that he could produce; yet men and machinery would stand idle because of the lack of profits. If this should be the case, wage claims would have to be controlled by the same means as those by which any other prices are controlled.

Price control and credit expansion to increase purchasing power will not necessarily remove unemployment and other frictional disturbances, if the various sectors of the economy are not subject under the same control. If, for example, retail prices should be subject to control but not wholesale and producer prices, the retailer might be forced out of business for lack of profits. If the price of manufactured goods should be subject to control but not that of raw materials, the manufacturer might suffer the same fate. Price control, as we have said, will administer justice only if all concerned are equally affected. Wage claims constitute prices and, as such, must be subject to the same regulations as any other prices. It does not mean that they must be controlled by the direct method of setting arbitrary wage rates. It means, rather, that the control commission must possess the authority to determine wages, commensurate with any other prices, in the event that such is necessary to ensure full employment.

There is every reason to believe, however, that eventually the question concerning what belongs to whom will be amicably settled between management and labor, and that no government control of wages will be necessary. There are a number of circumstances supporting this conclusion, such as the gradually improved understanding between the two traditional enemies, the trend toward profit sharing, the more rational approach toward wage settlements, etc. But what is of particular interest here is that the new condition of price stability under price control will contribute immensely to the faculty of understanding which is necessary for improved labor-management relations. It will compel labor to base wage demands on productivity, not on rising prices. Today wage demands are often based on an increased cost of living. The workingman argues that since prices are gradually rising, his real wages are being reduced, and, according to the escalator clause, he is justified in claiming higher wages. Many wage battles, in fact, are fought on this issue. And, naturally, since the employer is compelled to pay higher wages he feels himself justified in raising prices to compensate for the increased cost, whereupon the working-man again feels justified in claiming higher wages, ad infinitum. In this manner prices and wages continue their reciprocal climbs, each rise giving cause for another rise.

With the price level stabilized this vicious escalator condition will not obtain. Each dollar will retain generally the same purchasing value (even granting that perfection in this respect is not possible), and each increase in nominal wages and salaries will constitute a corresponding increase in real incomes. With this understanding in mind the wage earner must seek cause for higher wages on increased productivity rates, and must prove on this ground that he is entitled to a bigger share. Under these conditions it should be possible, also, to work out some permanent agreement by which wages are tied to productivity, taking account, of course, of capital investment and other pertinent matters. But whatever the case may be, it seems reasonable that this wage-determination problem is a matter which can be settled between management and labor without the direct intervention of any government agency.

5. The Honor System

Those who fear price control are in all certainty taking a darker than necessary view of this control measure. The fact is that price control need not be unpleasant or compulsive, provided that the plan in general attains a reasonable degree of success. In the beginning, undoubtedly, strict regulations must be applied to prevent non-compliance, since it would be overoptimistic to assume that complete confidence in the project could immediately be obtained. Assuming, however, that price stability and full employment have been achieved and fully recognized, the obligation to hold a level of prices should not cause a serious disagreement. We even tolerate taxation, when we know that this measure is necessary. There is the element of reason and fair play in human activity. Oftentimes a person will refrain from raising the price of his products or his merchandise, even when he could do so without losing the sale, because he does not want to profit at the expense of his regular customers. During the Second World War the Just Price Regulations applied in the United States in conjunction with the GMPR constituted an honor system, no more and no less, designed to compel businessmen to resist the temptation of raising prices for fear of being branded profiteers, yet these regulations were surprisingly effective in preventing price inflation. It is quite certain, also, that if the program of price stability and full employment has proved successful for a number of years or decades and the businessman is fully conscious that if he raises his prices above the level demanded by price stability he will go against the wishes of the public and against the interest of democracy, he will resist the temptation. This means that under the best of circumstances price control could consist only or mainly in a program of government inspection, or in the compilation of price indexes for the purpose of ascertaining that price stability is maintained.

We could not trust, however, that an honor system by itself would be effective for any length of time, unless it was based on the solid foundation of direct control. A car might follow the road for a short distance even without anyone holding the steering wheel, but eventually it would veer off to the side; and in order to keep it on the road, one would have to give the wheel at least an occasional turn to the right or to the left. So, also a pure honor system would undoubtedly be effective in holding the price level for a limited period even under a purchasing power level which would otherwise cause prices to rise, but if it is to be satisfactory as a permanent institution, it must be supplemented by a system of direct control sufficient to correct any irregularity that might appear. The price control commission must assume the ultimate responsibility of maintaining price stability, even if this should involve placing of the price tags on each commodity. It may delegate as much of this responsibility as it sees fit to private firms, but it must not under any circumstances allow pricing privileges which would start a vicious spiral of price increases; for upon the success of price control will rest the success of the whole program of credit expansion and full employment. It must retain the prerogative of price control, and it may sometimes be called upon to bring to justice those who do not comply with legitimate pricing practices. A purchasing power level sufficient to balance distribution would ordinarily cause prices to rise; and if an honor system is not effective enough to check this rise, the commission must take other such measures as will be adequate and appropriate at the time in question. An occasional rollback of prices can be expected.

It would undoubtedly be possible to raise the purchasing power and relieve the distributive problem to some extent without the implementation of strict price control, that is by establishing a closer tie between business, labor, and the government, with frequent negotiations and consultations so that each knows what the other plans to do. This can be seen in a country such as Sweden, where the government is in close partnership with business and labor. The intensity of the price struggle is comparative. There is no such thing as absolute freedom or absolute irresponsibility in the setting of prices. In any country or under any social environment the individual feels some responsibility in limiting price and wage claims; but this feeling may be more pronounced in some countries and under some environments than in others depending on the consciousness of those whom the pricing action concerns. If the individual should feel that the government and the public in general are fully conscious of his action, or if he should feel that he is a member of a larger body of businessmen or consumers whose interest it is to maintain price stability, he is more likely to voluntarily hold his price, even under a comparatively high level of purchasing power. Strict control, however, is irreplaceable and in the future, the only logical course of events, because it affords full control of purchasing power and makes it possible to constantly balance demand and distribution at the optimum level. It also ensures a fixed standard of value.

CHAPTER VII

CREDIT AND CREDIT CONTROL

1. Obsolete Theory of Money

There is perhaps no other subject of equal importance that is more widely misunderstood or about which more public illusion exists than the subject of money, or monetary credit. Even though money constitutes one of the most vital elements in our everyday economic life, the lifeblood of our economy, few will comprehend its true essence. What money is, what it stands for, how it comes into being, and how it is increased or decreased—these are subjects which baffle a great many people. Even the students of economics and the men engaged in various financial posts have a difficulty comprehending all the aspects of money.

The most common money illusion in our day is the commodity or material object concept which still occupies the minds of many people even in a credit economy, the reason being, of course, that the mind accepts material images more readily than immaterial things. It is comparatively easy to understand a commodity which can be seen and touched and stacked up the one over the other, such as pieces of gold or silver, bricks of tobacco or other objects, which used to be our medium of exchange. Credit is not as tangible and easy to understand as commodities. It cannot be seen or touched. All that we can see are the papers on which it is recorded, and we must use our imagination as to what the element consists of.

Credit, however, is not a difficult subject to understand. The confusion is caused by the absence of any generally expounded theory pertaining to monetary credit. Our monetary theories are based on conditions existing a century ago. Despite the fact that practically one hundred per cent of the money now in existence is in the form of credit which is distributed in wages, salaries and other income and which gives the creditor access to marketed goods and services, we fail to accept money as a medium of distribution. The student of economics is still being told the old absurdity that the monetary unit is a small quantity of gold or silver and that this unit serves as a standard of value. We still retain a monstrous gold reserve as a backing for our currency, even though the abundance of goods in the nation's market has long since made this reserve redundant. We still print on the face of the paper note a promise that does not make sense, even though it is abundantly clear to anyone that this credit is meant to afford access to goods and services.

The reason for this delayed theoretical recognition is that we find ourselves today in the midst of a revolutionary transition from one system to another, not only in the matter of money but also in the matter of economic exchange itself. Our money system has been or is being converted from a commodity basis to a credit basis, while exchange is being converted from a system based on direct trade to a system based on deposits and withdrawals. This change in our economic structure is gradual but unmistakable, and the uncertainty of today is caused by the fact that we cannot accept fully the one theoretical basis or the other. We have progressed far enough away from the commodity medium and direct trading to make these systems appear logical bases for our present economy, and yet we have not progressed far enough to base our theory on deposit, credit and withdrawal. In many instances our theory lags behind our practical accomplishments; and if we are to understand and deal effectively with the problems of today, we must first of all recognize in theory what has already been accomplished in practice.

2. Direct Trade

Direct trade between individuals or private parties is not confined to an age gone by; it can occur under the most modern conditions, just as self-help activities in the home may take place at any stage of our economic development. The exchange system today, however, is basically intermediate, whereas a couple of centuries ago economic exchange was executed mainly by the direct trade method.

Barter is the simplest and most original form of direct trade. It is performed without the aid of any social organization, and there is no intermediary or middleman involved. The goods that are traded pass directly from the ownership of the one person to the ownership of the other, and the terms of the transaction are negotiated each time a deal is made. If the one person had a goat, the other a quantity of tea, the two would settle the question of how much tea the goat was worth; and when both were satisfied, they would trade; and the transaction would be complete in all respects with no further obligation between them.

The invention of money marked the beginning of exchange organization. This invention, however, did not change the principle of direct trade upon which exchange transactions were executed. It facilitated trade in that it provided a standard for the evaluation of the commodities traded, but it did not materially change the method of trading. If we follow the history of the development of money, we will find that a great many commodities at some time or another have been used as money. A certain commodity, such as tea or tobacco, would at some time become more acceptable than others, and would be used as a standard for the evaluation of other commodities. This commodity would retain its utility, and would trade for other commodities on an equal value basis precisely as under original barter. The two trading parties would still become the owners of each other's commodities, estimated to have the same value, whether the one was in the nature of a money commodity or not.

The development of stores, or a market place, constituted another step in the organization of exchange. But even this step did not change the original concept of direct trade, so long as the goods in this market remained private or personal property and the money consisted of a commodity of intrinsic value equal to the value of the goods for which it traded. The producer selling a commodity in this market would still make a complete trade. He would relinquish the ownership of his commodity and would receive in exchange another commodity—gold, silver, shells—of equal value. The dealer would relinquish the ownership of the gold and would become the owner of the producer's commodity. This method of exchange would still be direct trade between private owners, more or less indistinguishable from barter. There would be no debt or credit relation between seller and buyer. Each would retain precisely what belonged to him after the deal was closed.

3. Indirect Trade

Today economic exchange cannot be described as a direct trade proposition between private owners. The person who today sells his labor or his products in the market does not make a complete trade with any one person or party; rather, he makes a deposit. The credit he receives in return has no value in itself. It simply certifies to the fact that the creditor made a contribution to marketed goods and that he now is entitled to draw other goods in return. When these other goods have been drawn and the credit relinquished, then a complete exchange has taken place. This is indirect or intermediate trade, a system basically different from the original barter or direct trade system. It is, in fact, a system of deposit and withdrawal, even if it is not yet recognized theoretically as such.

The difference between the two systems may be further clarified if we consider the function of exchange from the standpoint of the objective of the exchange transaction. Economic exchange, as we know, is an exchange of speciality for variety, that is, an exchange of a specific contribution of labor or products for the free-choice equivalent among the multitude of goods and services produced by others. Under the direct trade system the person who undertook to exchange his speciality for variety would make two complete trade transactions. First he would trade his speciality for money, a complete trade in itself. Second he would trade the money for other goods, another complete trade. Under the intermediate system of today, he would make only one complete trade transaction to accomplish the same objective. First he would trade his speciality for a paper which entitled him to claim goods of his free choice from the market. This first act constitutes the depository or contributory portion of the exchange transaction. Next he would withdraw his selection of other goods and relinquish his credit. After this second part of the transaction is over, the exchange of speciality for variety is complete.

4. The Common Market Reserve

This new concept calls for the recognition of a number of important generalizations pertaining to economic exchange. In the first place, the goods contained in the general market cannot be considered the private or personal property of the dealer in whose possession these goods are held. These goods, in fact, must be considered a common exchange reserve as a basis for credit and exchange. Each person who has contributed in some capacity to marketed goods or who has for one reason or another received or is in possession of monetary credit has a rightful claim on this reserve. The public representative in control of credit and distribution must have full distributive right to the market inventory. The dealer or salesman in whose possession marketed goods are held cannot claim absolute ownership of these goods any more than the banker can claim absolute ownership of the money deposited with him. Just as the banker has accepted a responsibility in holding the depositor's money until claimed, so the dealer or middleman has accepted a responsibility in holding marketed goods until these goods are claimed by the rightful owner, the creditor.

This concept of inventory ownership should not be construed as a limiting factor on the dealers right to his merchandise or on his position as a private dealer. Any dealer or merchant who has invested his own funds in merchandise on his premises must, of course, retain his personal rights to these goods. He must have the right to protect them as his own and refuse to part with them until payment has been realized or assured. It implies, however, that his right to the merchandise is limited, that there are certain ownership rights which he cannot by any moral standards claim.

The goods which pass through the market from producer to consumer constitute the total real income of the people of the nation. The money we receive in respect to our productive contributions is not the real income. This money is the papers or credits which entitle us to claim our real income in kind from the general market. It would be preposterous to assume, then, that these goods should be absolute property of the distributors alone and that the remainder of the population should have no ownership claim to them. It seems more logical to assume that each person who possesses monetary credit, producer or distributor, is the owner of marketed goods up to the limit of his credit and has the unequivocal right to claim these goods in full at any time he desires to do so. The distributor can claim financial right, but he cannot claim distributive right. He cannot hinder or thwart the distribution of these goods to the ultimate consumer.

The concept of a common market inventory as a basis for our money and exchange systems is perhaps the most fundamental principle that can be applied in a free enterprise economy. To the individual producer or worker, or to any other economic unit, company, corporation, firm, this all-goods reserve becomes the center and medium through which all economic exchange is executed, a general depository into which the specialities are entered and from which selected varieties are withdrawn. To the monetary authority this reserve becomes the basis of credit, the goods varieties against which monetary credit is issued, superseding the gold reserve as the backing for the currency. To the price control agency it becomes the field of operation, the place of business where the most careful work and study must be performed in order to attain the objectives of price control. To the fiscal agency in control of distribution it becomes the public treasury.

In an economy in which prices as well as credit must be strictly controlled to maintain purchasing power, it would seem justified to grant interest-free government loans to dealers or others as an aid to inventory accumulation, considering that with these control measures in effect the market inventory must in many respects be considered public property. Price control, in the first place, will make it necessary for the public agent to keep in very close contact with the market and to prescribe price changes whenever necessary. Credit control to balance production and distribution will make it necessary to regard the market inventory as the public treasury and the basis for public finance. It seems reasonable, therefore, that the government should compensate distributors and others in possession of marketed goods with interest-free loans up to the value of their respective inventories.

Marketed goods might be defined as undistributed national income, and as such they belong to each and every citizen in proportion to his rate of income. If we should divide the population into three income groups, producers, distributors and government workers, and assume that the proportion of the national income going to these group was 60 per cent, 25 per cent and 15 per cent respectively, the ownership of marketed goods could then be conferred on these groups according to these percentages; that is, 60 per cent of the current market inventory would belong to producers (and manufacturers), 25 per cent would belong to distributors, and 15 per cent to the government. The proposition that marketed goods must be regarded as a common national reserve implies that these goods cannot be subject to private or personal ownership until they are distributed to the ultimate consumer. It implies also that the public representative must assume the authority to protect the interest of each income group in regard to these goods, a task which it accomplishes through the maintenance of price and credit control.

5. The Direct Title Currency

Another generalization whose theoretical recognition is long overdue is that the currency should carry a direct promise of goods and services. What other promise could be more logical to place on the face of the paper note, considering that the purpose of a currency is to give the bearer access to the marketed goods and services which he is entitled to? The person who has currency in his possession can be assumed to have contributed in some capacity to the goods marketed and is therefore fully entitled to claim his share of marketed goods in return. He has made a deposit in the common market reserve, and the credit he receives in recognition of the deposit must give him undisputed right to withdraw his equity in other goods. The most logical thing to do in the immediate economic planning ahead is to print on the paper note a direct promise of goods in the open market.

Today we have a currency which carries on its face a promise of nothing more and nothing else than the currency itself, perhaps in another form. It does not promise anything that we might be willing to purchase, or anything for which we accept the currency. All that it promises is a renewal of itself or, at best, another form of itself. The American dollar note, for instance, carries a promise of one dollar in silver, implying that the note can be exchanged for coin, if brought to the bank. The Canadian dollar note, however, simply carries a promise of "One Dollar," which might mean another dollar note, perhaps a little newer and cleaner than the one exchanged. Even authorities admit that these promises no longer make sense, yet they continue to reappear. The feeling is that no one will bother to read the promise anyway, so it does not matter.

These promises — or the lack of them — constitute another reminder of the uncertainty and lack of theoretical foundation on which our credit system operates. It shows a wavering between a commodity basis and a credit basis on the one hand and between a direct trade system and a deposit and withdrawal principle on the other. The paper note was originally meant to be accepted in place of gold which could be drawn from the bank at any time that the bearer so desired. The person who accepted this currency, then, became the owner of gold which was held for him in safety deposit at the bank, and when he made purchases in the market he traded this gold for the goods and services he purchased. This action was still direct trade, a trading of gold for goods and services and goods and services for gold. Today, however, gold payments have long since been suspended, and yet we fail to recognize marketed goods as the basis of credit. This leaves the currency theoretically without a backing, based on nothing but itself.

This timid money policy in our modern day does not seem consistent with accepted standards of logic. It is implicit, especially since the suspension of gold payments, that the market inventory constitutes even now the true basis of our credit system, yet we fail to recognize the fact. It would appear from here that marketed goods are still considered personal property and that the government has no right to issue credit against them or to indicate in any way that the currency is meant to give access to goods, let alone any set value in such goods. It implies that the government can issue a currency but cannot designate this currency to the purpose for which it is issued. The currency, apparently, is meant to be accepted on its own merit and at the valuation at which dealers from their own discretion will decide to confer upon it. This policy indicates also that we are still leaning hesitatingly toward a system of direct trade or barter by which goods and services are traded for paper whose valuation is achieved through scarcity.

Changing the promise on the face of the paper note from a promise of silver or paper to a promise of goods and services will not make the currency more acceptable. The present currency is already fully accepted. In fact, each person in the Western world is endeavoring his best to push goods and services on the other person in return for credit, and to improve on this acceptability would be difficult. Nor will a direct title currency augment the power of the government to issue credit; the government is already in full control of the nation's numerical credit volume and could increase this volume to any extent it saw fit. A direct title currency, however, will place the nation's credit in its rightful position as a direct medium of distribution. It will establish that the person who has accepted this currency in recognition for an economic contribution or for any other reason or right has the absolute right not only to claim goods and services but also to demand that these goods and services be delivered in full. It will establish that the government or public representative must possess the full right to issue credit against goods in the general market and also to designate the value of this credit through the control of prices.

The doctrine that the dealer or distributor should possess the freedom to raise or determine the price of the marketed goods in his possession does not appear logical from the point of view of the creditor's ownership right. This would seem to indicate that the distributor should have the right to determine the value of the monetary unit as well as to lower or allocate at his own discretion the creditor's share of marketed goods. This would be comparable to a banker's right to lower at his own discretion a creditor's deposit account. Our real deposit in this day of specialization is not in the bank but in the market; and it seems equally important, if not more so, that this deposit should be ensured by legislative action. During the barter era the freedom to raise prices might be deemed more justified, considering that both buyer and seller had a commodity of intrinsic value. But today the buyer has only a paper whose value is conditioned solely on the nation's price structure; and if we assume, as we must, that legislation is designed to administer justice in monetary dealings, we must admit that the prerogative of pricing cannot justifiably be bestowed on individuals in pursuit of personal gain.

6. Credit versus Credit Instruments

The functional attributes which have been traditionally conferred on money, evidently with a commodity currency in view, are those of standard of value and medium of exchange; and these attributes are often erroneously applied to the present currency, even as it exists today. This again is a reminder that our money theories are lagging behind our practical accomplishments. With the money system purely on a credit basis, and especially under a system of controlled distribution, such a division of the monetary qualities would not make sense. In the first place, credit cannot serve as a standard and measure of value any more than a meal ticket can serve as a measure of calories. Credit constitutes a title to goods which are already measured through the process of price control. In the second place, the term medium of exchange is not the most appropriate to use in reference to credit savings. It would be more appropriate, we would assume, to refer to credit as unclaimed real income and to reserve the term medium of exchange for the common market inventory, as this reserve is the medium through which all economic exchange is executed.

There is one monetary division, however, which cannot escape our attention. It is the division into credit and credit instruments, the one representing title to or ownership of marketed goods, the other representing the papers or other material objects on which the credit is recorded. It would hardly seem necessary to point out the difference between these two elements, yet there is a widespread confusion on the matter. Traditionally we have been taught to accept money as a commodity, and consequently have lumped the two elements together into one object; and this material concept of money has carried through even in a credit system, and constitutes the greatest cause of the money illusion. To a great many people money is still a material object, and this is an illusion which is difficult to eradicate. Some writers refer to gold or silver certificates, token money, metallic money, and money of account as so many different types of money, without any mention of whether this list refers to credit or to credit instruments. To master the subject of money it is necessary that we should have a clear conception of the difference between credit and credit instruments.

The distinction between the two elements may be illustrated by some simple comparisons. Thus, for instance, credit is an intangible quality; it has no weight or bulk, and cannot be seen or touched. Credit instruments, on the other hand, may consist of various material substances. Credit instruments, again, may take various shapes and forms, such as notes, coins, checks, drafts, money orders, and bank deposit files. Credit, however, has only one form; it constitutes ownership of unclaimed goods and services, and is the same irrespective of who the creditor may be or what forms of papers or other media he may present to prove the existence of this credit.

Credit may conceivably exist without credit instruments to prove its existence; but what we are concerned with at present is registered or recognized credit, that is, credit recorded in bank deposit ledgers, on notes, coins, or otherwise.

When calculating the volume of money in existence in the nation, we must not confuse credit with credit instruments. What we want to know is how many units of credit the people of the nation possess, or how many units of goods they possess title to, not how many papers are available to record this credit. This latter variable might reveal an entirely different figure, since notes and coins may or may not represent or embody credit. They do when held by individuals, families or private parties, but not when held by such institutions as the banking system, the mint, the treasury, or any branch of the federal government.

To illustrate this point let us consider the case that a person is in possession of one thousand dollars in monetary credit, all of which he holds in the form of savings deposits at the bank. The thousand dollars testifies to the fact that he is the owner of one thousand price units of marketed goods which he may claim in the general market at any time that he finds it convenient to do so. If now he should demand cash in the form of paper notes for his thousand dollars and close his deposit account, he would have a different means of proving that he is the owner of the thousand goods units, but his credit would still be one thousand dollars, no more and no less. If he should subsequently exchange these notes for coins, travelers' cheques or some other media, he would still have precisely one thousand dollars. He would have various means by which to prove that he is the owner of one thousand dollars, but he cannot hereby change the figure of his credit. These various papers or instruments do not constitute money or credit in themselves; they are simply the means by which credit is recorded; and whenever one credit instrument is exchanged for another, credit is transferred from the one to the other.

The same is true when the nation as a whole is considered. Suppose, for instance, that the people of the nation should possess a total of ten billion dollars, implying that they would possess claims against marketed goods up to this amount. This money volume, then, would remain at ten billion dollars irrespective of the forms of instruments which were used to record it. Changing from bank accounts to cash or from cash to bank accounts would change the manner in which the credit was recorded, but would not in any way change the numerical volume of the credit. If the people should decide to draw all their money from the bank in the form of cash and close all deposit accounts, the central bank would necessarily be called upon to print and distribute to the various banks a huge additional volume of bills to meet the demand; but when this process was completed, the volume of credit in people's possession would still be only ten billion dollars. The same would be the case if the creditors should reverse the process and deposit all these bills in the bank in favor of savings accounts. The banking system would then hold at least ten billion dollars in paper notes, but these notes would no longer embody credit, since the credit has now been transferred from them to the deposit ledger. The nation could not possibly transfer the ten billion dollars from the bills to the savings accounts and still retain the credit which was represented by the bills. Paper notes held by the banking system do not represent credit. As soon as they enter the bank, credit is transferred from them to the deposit account, and these notes become idle papers with no more significance than check blanks.

7. The Transfer of Credit

Credit is transferred from one creditor to another or from one account to another by either of two common means, checks and cash. The check, which is very common on this continent of America, is a simple instrument requesting the banker to transfer a specified sum from one account to another. It must carry the name of the person from whose account the credit is to be drawn as well as that of the person whose account is to be credited. It must also specify the exact amount to be transferred. The receiver, or drawee, will present the check to his bank and have the specified amount entered to his account, whereupon the check is forwarded to the drawer's bank and his account deducted from. The transfer then is complete.

When a certified check is drawn, credit is transferred from the drawer's account to the check before it is presented to the drawee.

A certified check, therefore, embodies credit commensurate with cash, and upon presentation to the bank this credit is transferred to the drawee's account whereupon the check becomes invalid.

It would be quite possible to transfer credit from one account to another without the use of the check, provided that the banker could otherwise be informed of the particulars involved and authorized to proceed with the transfer. This could be done, for instance, if both drawer and drawee had their accounts at the same bank. The banker could then, upon request, produce the two accounts and deduct the specified sum from the one account and add it to the other. The reason for using the check is partly that the accounts of the two parties concerned may be held in different banks located in different parts of the country, and partly that the signatures of the drawer and the drawee make the cheque a legal document, thus authorizing the banker to proceed with the transfer.

The second common method of transferring credit is by means of cash (notes and coins). Notes and coins are comparable with certified checks issued in fixed amounts, and may be transferred in similar manner. Thus, if Mr. A wishes to pay one hundred dollars to Mr. B, he may proceed to draw this sum in cash from the bank. And in doing so, credit is transferred from his account to the cash which, by this action, becomes valid. Mr. B, upon receiving this cash, may, if he so wishes proceed to deposit it in the bank and have the credit transferred to his account. As soon as this is done, the cash again becomes idle papers with no credit representation.

Cash is the most convenient means by which to transfer credit from one person or party to another, and is used in the majority of credit transactions, especially when small amounts are involved. However, since it embodies credit and is payable to bearer, it provides a temptation to theft, and its use should be limited to comparatively small amounts. Checks, which are safer and less negotiable, should be used whenever larger transactions are involved.

Those who advocate the abolition of money may not possess a very clear picture of what such an undertaking would actually involve, and it is anybody's privilege to conjecture its implication. If by the abolition of money is meant the discontinuation of the use of cash, we are ready to admit that the project would be within the range of possibilities. The purpose of cash, as we know, is to transfer credit from person to person in the settlement of debt or otherwise; but the banking system is already performing this function whenever requested to do so through the medium of the check; and it would be quite possible to extend this service to include all credit transactions. It would undoubtedly create a measure of encumbrance, but it would be possible. It would require each person to pay by cheque instead of by cash for all his purchases and for all his monetary settlements, and it would require the banking system to transfer the stipulated sums of all these settlements.

The reason why this is not done is, of course, that the transfer of credit from one account to another requires time and would not be economical when small amounts are involved. The accounts of the drawer and the drawee are often located in different banks and in different localities of the country, and whenever a check is drawn these accounts must somehow be found and the adjustments made. Generally the drawee's account is first produced and the specified sum added. The cheque then passes through the clearinghouse to the drawer's bank where his account is deducted from. But if the millions of daily credit transactions which now are handled by cash should be made by means of drawing checks, the banking system would be burdened with a tremendous task. Mr. A, for instance, would purchase a newspaper and pay by check, and the banker would transfer five cents from Mr. A's account to that of the newsstand. Mr. B would purchase a bus ticket and pay by check, and the banker would deduct ten cents from Mr. B's account and add the same sum to the account of the transportation company. Others would buy an apple, a pack of cigarettes, a restaurant meal; and each time a check would be drawn, and the banker would have to transfer the nominal amounts from drawer's to drawee's account. The clearinghouse would receive truckloads of checks and would busy itself clearing odd sums between millions of accounts; and the cost of transferring would often be higher than the amounts transferred. It is not likely, therefore, that in the foreseeable future we will do without cash. Notes and coins embody credit, and all that is necessary is to hand them over to the vender, and the credit transaction is complete. Perhaps the future will bring some invention which will simplify the transfer of credit between the various accounts, but until then we must content ourselves with notes and coins.

8. The Creation of Credit

When saying that credit is being transferred from one account to another we are not consistent with the most discriminate semasiology. We would come nearer to the truth by saying that credit is being withdrawn or eliminated from the one account and that new credit is added to the other. Credit is an intangible quality, and there is absolutely nothing that we can lift or move from one place to another. Even if the banker should have the two accounts in front of him, he could not possibly remove anything from the one and transfer over to the other. What he enters into the one account is not necessarily that which he deducts from the other, except that the figures correspond. By deducting from and adding to credit accounts he is in fact eliminating credit as well as creating new credit, and the volume of credit in the nation is thereby affected, even if this is only for a very limited duration. If he has the two accounts in front of him and deducts, let us say, one hundred dollars from the one account before adding the same sum to the other, there would be, other things being the same, one hundred dollars less registered credit in existence, at least for a few seconds until the other account had been credited. If he should add to the one account before deducting from the other, the opposite would be the case.

The effect on the money volume caused by these addings and deductings may seem insignificant. We must remember, however, that the lapse of time between addings and deductings is not as a rule a matter of seconds but a matter of days. Generally when a check is drawn on an account and handed to a person in payment of debt, this person will proceed to the bank and have his account credited with the specific amounts, or he will draw cash. The check then is forwarded to the bank in which the drawer's account is registered, and the corresponding amount is deducted. But the time it takes to complete this transaction will depend among other things on the proximity of the drawer's bank. If this bank is located in another part of the country, it may take several days, perhaps weeks, before the drawer's account is debited. And during this time the person who received the credit may have paid part or all of it to others, either in the form of cash or checks, and these people, in turn, may have paid it to still others, so that this credit may have passed through many hands before and until finally the original drawer's account is debited. Any person drawing a check, therefore, is creating new credit which remains in existence for at least a temporary duration. But when we consider the fact that millions of checks are drawn each day in varying amounts, we must admit that millions of dollars are permanently in existence as a result of these delayed transactions.

A more effective method of creating credit, however, is by taking or extending bank loans. Whenever a person borrows money from a commercial bank his credit account is added to just as it would be if he made a deposit; and, in contrast to the process of a credit transfer, this credit is not deducted from any other account. It is new credit created at the time the loan is made, a new addition to the volume of money in circulation. It is the understanding, of course, that this credit is to be deducted from the borrower's own account at the expiration of the term of the loan. During this time, however, there is in existence money which did not exist before, money which circulates in the ordinary manner from person to person or from account to account. When at maturity the loan is paid the borrower's account is debited, and the credit passes out of existence. Considering, however, that a multitude of loans are outstanding at all times, the credit circulating as a result of these loans amounts to billions. And this credit constitutes in large measure the monetary volume of the present day.

During the commodity-money era the task of making new money involved certain difficulties. It might involve, for instance, the mining of gold and the minting of this gold into specie. Credit, on the other hand, could be created by anyone who could write his name on a check, provided that this credit was recognized by the banking system. Generally, of course, any person's credit making is limited to the extent of his own credit account, unless he receives a loan. A bank could create or issue any amount of credit through its lending operations were it not for the fact that its cash reserves constitute a limiting factor. According to central bank regulations a member bank must maintain a proportion of cash or central bank deposits which does not fall below a set percentage of its outstanding loans. These regulations prevent an undue inflation of credit.

A bank's lending power, however, is not limited to existing credit, either cash or customer deposits. If cash was not demanded or used and all credit transactions were performed through the medium of the check, it would be quite possible for the bank to "lend" any amount of credit without having even a dollar in its possession, for what a bank lends is little more than its services.

We might illustrate the above by an example. Suppose that there was no money of any form in existence, no notes or coins, and no bank accounts. Suppose, however, that a banking system existed, fully staffed and fully ready to serve its customers. Under these conditions, then, a prospective borrower, let us say John Smith, proceeds to the bank and requests a loan of $20,000. If the banker finds that John Smith is absolutely reliable and solvent, he will grant the loan. In doing so he opens a deposit account in John Smith's name amounting to $20,000, and the loan has been made. John Smith may now draw checks against this account up to the limit of $20,000. And these checks may be paid to a large number of people, who may open checking accounts in their own names and who, in turn, may draw checks against these accounts to pay to others. Thus, the new credit will pass from person to person and from account to account in the ordinary manner. There is now $20,000 in circulation just as sound as any money that we use at present, while John Smith owes a debt of $20,000 to the bank.

But let us suppose now that a second person, for instance John Jones, proceeds to the bank to borrow $20,000. Granted the loan, he also will receive a checking account of $20,000 and will proceed to draw checks against this account to pay for the various commodities and services he purchases. There is now $40,000 in circulation which did not exist before, while the two borrowers owe a debt to the banks of $40,000.

A third person, and a fourth, and a fifth, also proceed to the bank each to borrow $20,000; and the money in circulation is increased to $100,000, while the five borrowers owe a debt of $100,000.

More people head for the bank to borrow money, and the deposits grow to a million, and ten million, and a hundred million, and a billion, and ten billions. And by this time accounts have been opened by people throughout the land, with millions of credit transactions being a daily routine, while the borrowers owe a debt to the banking system amounting to ten billion dollars.

The time has now arrived when John Smith, the original borrower, must pay his debt to the bank. Before doing so he must make certain that he has a balance of at least $20,000 in his deposit account. This requirement assured, the banker will deduct $20,000 from his account, and the debt is paid. By this time there is no longer ten billion dollars in circulation; this volume has been reduced by $20,000.

But the time has come, also, for John Jones to pay his debt to the bank, and when this has been done the money in circulation has been reduced by $40,000. When all the borrowers have paid their debts to the banking system, every last dollar in circulation has also disappeared, and the nation is back where it started from.

The above example illustrates the conditions on which our present money system is based. All money in circulation today is in the form of credit backed by a corresponding volume of debt. When debt increases, credit also increases; and when debt is reduced, credit is also reduced. If all debts should be paid, credit would also disappear. What would be left of our whole monetary structure are the silver and copper coins which still exist in the form of an intrinsic value commodity and which constitute perhaps one per cent of our monetary volume.

9. Corporate Debt

This debt-based money proposition may appear startling to those who visualize money as a stockpile of material objects; but it is entirely logical, considering what is meant by credit. To have credit implies to have something owing, but we cannot have things owing to us unless someone (person or party) owes them. We have nothing owing to us from some other planet, nor have we under the present system any common reserve or pool in which we can claim our share of ownership. All goods for which our credit tenders are considered private property; and if some of us are to have credit, or title to goods, some others must hold these goods and be directly or indirectly in debt on account of them. Debt may be defined as the obligation to return something borrowed or to return or deliver something belonging to others. Credit (in a monetary sense) may be defined as the ownership and promised release (on request) of something held by others. Obviously the two must correspond in nominal volume, the one being as essential to our economic life as the other.

There are, of course, a multitude of debt and credit relations whose expansion or contraction does not affect the money volume. This is expressly so when already existing credit is concerned. If Peter borrows a dollar from Paul, there is no change in the credit volume, since this dollar already existed. The only difference is that Peter has the dollar instead of Paul. The same is true whenever existing credit is borrowed, whether this is done through savings banks, credit unions, investment companies or any other financial intermediaries, or through the sale of bonds to the general public. Such borrowings may be instrumental in speeding circulation in so far as the borrowers may readily proceed to spend the money whereas the lenders would not otherwise have done so, but it does not increase the volume of existing credit.

It makes credit available to the borrower, but it ties up credit from the lender. The kind of borrowing that increases the credit volume is the borrowing (through commercial banks or otherwise) which makes credit available to the one person or party without tying up or reducing the liquidity of any one else's credit.

Whenever things are borrowed, however, whether this be money or goods, and whenever goods are purchased on credit, there arise a creditor on the one hand and a debtor on the other, and the credit ascribed to the one cannot be greater than the debt ascribed to the other. If there were no debt, that is, if no one should hold in his possession things belonging to others, there could be no credit. The right to claim goods and services cannot be greater than the obligation to release or deliver these goods and services. To create credit, whether this be monetary or any other credit, someone must accept goods belonging to others and thereby contract a debt obligation, and the credit so created will be nominally the same as the debt obligation.

But whereas this debt-equals-credit equation must be generally accepted as true, we must not forget that the element of debt has a vastly different meaning when carried by a corporation than when carried by an individual. If all money-based debt should be carried by individuals, we would have a situation in which the debt in the hands of some people would equal the credit in the hands of others, the net credit volume of the nation being nil. In other words, some people would have more than nothing in monetary savings, others would have less than nothing to the same numerical extent, a rather dismal prospect. Increasing the credit volume under this condition would simply mean the widening of the debt-and-credit spread on either side of the zero mark, giving some people more credit and forcing others deeper into debt. When money-based debt is held by corporations, associations and government bodies, the people as individuals may have credit without debt. If all money-based debt should be held by the federal government, no individual or private party would need to be in debt on account of the existing credit volume; and this volume could be increased without burdening any one person or private company with the obligation of debt.

10. The Common Reserve Basis of Credit

A common market inventory as a backing for the nation's credit volume becomes the most logical institution in our present-day economic environment. It concentrates money-based debt obligations in the hands of a government commission in control of distribution, and it makes it possible for the public at large to realize debt-free credit. Credit is created by means of depositing specialities into a common pool from which other goods are withdrawn in the process of exchange. Without a common market reserve, that is, with marketed goods being considered private property in the hands of a million dealers, monetary credit must be created by means of creating private debt.

We might illustrate this circumstance by an example. Suppose that the nation consists of a hundred persons each of whom is in possession of one thousand dollars' worth of marketable goods which he desires to exchange for credit. Suppose also that there exists no previous debt and credit arrangement between the hundred persons. Under these circumstances credit could not possibly exist, since each person would hold precisely what belonged to him. In order to create credit they have two choices at their disposal: they may place the goods into the hands of one another or they may place them into a common reserve. If they pursue the first course of action, some of the hundred persons will hold more goods than they own and will be in debt; others will hold less than they own and will have credit. If, for instance, fifty of the hundred persons should place their thousand dollars of goods in the possession of the other fifty, this latter group would each hold two thousand dollars of goods and would have a debt of one thousand dollars. The other fifty would have no goods on hand, but would have one thousand dollars of credit each. If ninety of the hundred persons should place their goods in possession of the remaining ten, these ninety would each have one thousand dollars in credit, while the ten who had accepted the goods would have a combined debt of ninety thousand dollars. In either case, however, the volume of debt in the hands of the one group would equalize the credit in the hands of the other, the average or net credit between the hundred persons being nil.

But suppose now that they should pursue the second course of action and place all their goods into a common reserve under a common organization or dead-hand owner. In this case each of the hundred persons could have one thousand dollars of credit, and no one would carry a personal debt. The only debtor in this case would be the body of their own organization.

The explanation of this phenomenon is simple. We cannot have the goods as personal property and also have credit which entitles us to these goods. To have credit, as we have said, implies to have something owing to us, but before we can have things owing to us someone must owe them. As long as each and all of us hold precisely as many goods as belong to us, we cannot have credit. We must first dispose of our goods before we can have credit which entitles us to claim these goods. And there are only two ways in which we can do this: we can push the goods into the hands of one another and get one another's credit, or we can place them into a common pool and so receive title to them.

Considering that economic exchange is an exchange of specialities for varieties, it seems logical that the latter course should be the proper procedure. The specialities which we individually produce are of little or no value to us, and as long as we hold these we are prevented from coming in contact with the varieties which we need for our personal use. What could be more logical than a common depository into which the specialities may be disposed of and against which credit may be issued as direct title to other goods without creating personal debt obligations? To create credit by pushing the goods into the hands of one another is reminiscent of unorganized barter. Obviously, the establishment and recognition of a common market reserve as a basis of credit is the most logical institution and one which we must consider inevitable in the immediate economic planning ahead.

11. The Direct Issue of Credit

A common market reserve, furthermore, will revolutionize public finance in that it will establish direct issue and withdrawal of credit as the basic formula. Every dollar spent by the federal government in its current financing will be new credit issued at the time of payment, and every dollar taxed or brought in will be withdrawn as credit. This is true whether currency notes or checks are used, since credit instruments held by the central government do not represent credit. The central government, as a public institution, cannot possess monetary credit. It can possess credit instruments, but it cannot possess credit. Monetary credit can be held only by people as individuals or groups of individuals who are share owners in the general market reserve, not by an institution in possession of this reserve. The government representative in whose possession the market inventory can be considered held becomes the debtor through its obligation to redeem outstanding credit in marketed goods on demand; and whenever such credit is withdrawn through taxation or otherwise debt obligation is cancelled out, and the credit no longer exists. Money (monetary credit) will circulate and continue to exist whenever it passes through private hands, but when it enters the possession of the central government it ceases to exist, whereupon new credit and new debt obligations are created through further government expenditures.

This seeming departure from the traditional concept of public finance according to which pre-existing credit is used may be less radical than it first appears. When dealing with an intangible element such as credit it is sometimes difficult to determine what is new and what is pre-existent. Actually the credit paid out by the federal government even today is new credit created at the time of payment. In America, for instance, every dollar paid out by the Government through its ordinary expenditures is issued in the form of checks, and every dollar levied in taxes or other charges is received in the form of checks; and there is absolutely nothing that can be lifted or transferred from the one collection of checks to the other. The old checks are cancelled and destroyed as soon as the figures of credit they carry are recorded. The new checks represent new credit distributed to the various peoples who supply the goods and services needed by the government; and it would be quite possible for the government to discontinue taxation altogether and still continue to finance in the ordinary manner all its expenditures through the issue of checks, were it not for the fact that such a process would lead to a disastrous inflation of credit.

The traditional concept of public finance is that the government is levying from the public a specified rate of tax money which it uses to pay for its various expenditures, and if this money is not sufficient to meet needed expenditures it must resort to borrowings from the bank or from the public. This viewpoint is another reminder of the commodity or material-object illusion of money handed down from a time when money consisted of pure gold or other valuables. It is indicative of the idea that money must already exist before it can be paid out to anyone, that it cannot be made or created by the government or by anyone else. It implies, in other words, that money exists in a fixed volume which can neither be increased nor decreased, and that when the government imposes taxes it must necessarily levy from this limited volume, or else resort to borrowing.

This inflexibility or permanent-existence concept of money can be explained from the fact that the majority of credit transactions in today's economy are performed between individuals or groups of individuals who have no authority to issue credit but who must limit their finances to their own bank accounts or to strictly limited loans. If the whole national market, that is, all stores, wholesale and retail, should be socialized and operated by the government as one single store, we would in all probability attain an entirely different concept of money, a short-life concept, since credit, in this case, would be issued anew to the producer whenever he marketed goods, and whenever he purchased goods in the market, credit would cease to exist. Credit (or money) would exist only as long as the creditor held a deposit of goods in the common market reserve. It would be issued at the time of deposit and withdrawn at the time of withdrawal; and if deposits should exceed withdrawals, credit would increase; if withdrawals should exceed deposits, credit would decrease.

Since stores today and—as far as we can see—tomorrow remain private enterprises, credit cannot be directly issued upon the marketing of goods, nor will credit immediately cease to exist with the withdrawal of goods. The credit received by the dealer will exist in his possession until he parts with it. When entering the possession of the government, however, credit ceases to exist. Credit begins and ends at the government level; and whenever the outgo of credit from the government exceeds the inflow, the outstanding credit expands; whenever the inflow exceeds the outgo, credit contracts. Under Controlled Distribution, this balancing of government income and expenditure must become the principal method of credit control.

This does not preclude, by any means, the possibility of private or corporate debt as a basis of credit. A considerable proportion of the nation's credit may still be backed by private debt contracted by the issue of commercial bank loans, and the credit volume of the nation will naturally be affected by the expansion and contraction of this credit. It will be possible, also, to exercise a measure of credit control by adjusting the conditions on which bank loans are granted, that is, by adjusting cash requirements and interest rates, both of which are under the control of the central bank.

The ultimate control of credit, however, must be realized through the direct issue and withdrawal of credit by the fiscal authority in its ordinary function of public finance. Private loans cannot be depended on to supply the precise amount of credit necessary to balance distribution. The supply of credit is critical. The fiscal authority must remain in constant contact with the market; and if at any time the market inventory should show signs of becoming overabundant, this authority must take steps to expand credit. If the opposite condition should manifest itself, it must contract credit.

12. Unrestricted Credit Control

Another arrangement which will inevitably follow the establishment of a common market reserve and Controlled Distribution is that no debt or credit relation can exist between the government and the banking system. Undoubtedly the maintenance of budget figures showing government outgo and income of credit will be desirable, and in interest of this objective the banking system will serve in a valuable capacity. Any equivalent of a government bank account or bank credit standing, however, is redundant. The government, as we have said, will directly issue credit, thus becoming directly indebted to the individual creditor through its guarantee of redemption, and this debt is paid when the creditor claims his share of marketed goods. The government cannot at the same time be indebted to the bank in respect to the same credit. This credit is not borrowed or drawn from any account, debit or credit, nor is the credit received by the government added to or deposited in any account, except in so far as it serves a statistical purpose.

The purpose of bank accounts or bank credit standings such as those held by individuals or private parties is, of course, to restrict credit expansion. It would be physically possible for the individual, even without possessing a bank account, to issue almost any amount of credit, either through the medium of checks or paper notes, provided that this were permitted. The credit account prevents this credit inflation from taking place. The individual is restricted in his "credit making" to his own account or to strictly limited loans which must subsequently be repaid in credit, and if he should attempt to issue credit beyond this limit, his checks would not be recognized by the banking system. In this manner the bank performs the vital function of credit restriction.

If the individual dealer should issue credit or notes against his own merchandise only, that is, if the shoe dealer should issue notes against shoes in his own store, the baker issuing notes against bread and cake, the druggist issuing notes against drugs, etc., there would be no need for the bank to restrict credit. The dealer could then directly issue his notes without any bank loan and without even contacting or consulting the bank, since he would then assume full responsibility of redeeming his notes in his own merchandise. But since any notes or credit issued by anyone must give access to goods, not only in the issuer's own store, but in any store or distributive outlet in the nation, the individual could not possibly be free to make his own credit. Any such freedom would cause the credit volume to explode into astronomical figures in a matter of minutes.

The government commission whose duty it is to control credit, however, cannot itself be controlled or restricted in its credit issue by any other agency. This commission is already restricted in its credit issue by its obligation to maintain an optimum market reserve. It is issuing credit directly against the national market inventory, the inventory for which it is responsible; and even though it has a free hand in issuing credit, it is strictly limited in this issue; for any overissue, even small, might cause shortages of marketed goods. Its credit issue must be determined by the condition of the market, not by that of the bank. A government commission which was limited in its financing to its own credit account and which upon the exhaustion of this account would have to appeal to the bank or to the public for loans would not be in a position to control distribution. The commission in control of distribution must have undisputed control of credit.

Today there is a popular conception that when the government spends more than it takes in, the public debt will necessarily increase. If, for instance, it should tax a total of ten billions and spend eleven billions, the public debt would have increased by one billion. If by *debt* we mean the obligation to release marketed goods on demand, or the obligation to redeem the currency or the outstanding credit, this conception would make sense even under a system of Controlled Distribution, since the obligation to release marketed goods must at any one time equal the outstanding credit. But it is obvious that this debt is not what we generally refer to as public debt. There is no need for a public debt such as we know it. Deficit financing creates a larger outstanding credit volume and a larger volume of claims on marketed goods, but it does not under Controlled Distribution create the equivalent of today's public debt.

CHAPTER VIII

CONTROL OF DISTRIBUTION

The circumstance which must guide the action of the credit control commission under a system of price and credit control is, of course, the supply condition of the common market inventory. This inventory must be maintained at an optimum level, never oversupplied or undersupplied; and the national money supply or national money income must be balanced accordingly. Generally speaking, the national income must be so adjusted that goods are withdrawn from the market at the rate at which they are deposited, leaving the inventory unchanged. With the price level (or goods unit) stabilized, this income could not register a spectacular change from time to time, numerically speaking. It could change only with a change in productivity.

1. The Income-Price Equation

It would be possible, perhaps, to express in mathematical terms the maximum possible monetary income in any given production period relative to the national product. The basic theorem from which to proceed in arriving at this figure is that the total income should be equal to the total price of the goods produced. This simple criterion is based on the premise that it requires a unit of credit to redeem a unit of price. The pricing process, as we know, involves the divisioning of goods into equal units, each of which requires a monetary unit to redeem. As soon as goods are placed in the market at a price, no one can withdraw these goods without first redeeming the price with credit in corresponding amounts. It seems logical, therefore, that if we are to maintain a balanced distribution we must create monetary income at the same rate as we create price, or, in other words, we must create the power to release goods (from the market) at the rate at which we tie goods through the imposition of price. If we designate income with the letter I and prices with the letter P, we get $I = P$.

This rule, however, is conditioned upon two vital prerequisites, first, that the amount of goods to be distributed should always equal that marketed and, second, that the people in receipt of income should always spend as much as they receive. If both of these conditions should apply unreservedly, the income-equals-price equation would be correct. It is very unlikely, however, that such would be the case. In the first place, it is unlikely that the same amount of goods should always be distributed to the ultimate consumer as that which is produced. This would imply that the market inventory, the reserve of finished goods in the hands of dealers, producers and manufacturers, should always remain constant, never to be increased or decreased. It is more likely that this reserve will at some time or another be found inadequate or overabundant and that in order to correct the situation the income, on this account, will have to be slightly above or below the total price. In a country with an expanding economy the market reserve may have to be subject to a gradual expansion, and to allow for this expansion the income would have to be somewhat below the total price. If, for instance, the market reserve should require an increase of two per cent of the national turnover, the income, on this account, would have to be placed at 98 per cent of the total price, or if the total price of the goods marketed during a given period should be $100,000,000 according to the retail price quotations, the national income should be $98,000,000. Designating the increase in the national market reserve with the letter R, we get $I = P - R$.

The second exception to the rule involves the question of savings. Just as it is unlikely that the market reserve should always remain constant, so it is unlikely that the credit savings in the hands of the public will always remain the same, or that the people will always spend as much as they receive. If there should be a change in the volume of savings, or a difference in the total income and the total spendings, the national income would have to be adjusted so as to counteract this difference. If, for instance, 100,000,000 goods units (price units of goods) were to be distributed in a given period, we should distribute, not necessarily $100,000,000, but an income sufficient to induce people to purchase and withdraw from the market 100,000,000 price units of goods. If during the period the public should add $2,000,000 to their credit savings, the national income during the same period should be $102,000,000, or sufficient to supply the extra savings without affecting distribution. Designating savings with the letter S, we arrive at our complete equation: $I = P - R + S$.

2. Free versus Priced Goods

But whereas this equation is generally correct, we must not forget that the total price is not indicative of the total volume of goods. There is a great variety of goods, services and utilities which are not subject to price and cannot, therefore, command monetary income. They are such goods and services as roads, streets, bridges, parks, playgrounds, sewers, public buildings, schools, libraries, hospitals, medical care, education, police protection, fire protection, national defense, and a host of other services and utilities usually provided by federal, regional and local governments. These goods and services are just as valuable as those that are sold in the market, but they are not subject to price and, consequently, no monetary income can be distributed against them. Monetary income can be distributed only against such goods and services as are priced, or against the portion of the gross national product that is priced, whatever percentage of the national product this portion may represent. If eighty per cent of all goods and services should be priced, the remaining twenty per cent being free to enjoy without charge, the total money income could not be higher than the price value of the eighty per cent that was priced.

This reasoning becomes entirely logical when we consider that the only purpose for distributing monetary income is to release or free goods which are tied in the market by price. In a complete communist society in which all goods were distributed free of charge, there could be no such thing as monetary income, for the simple reason that there would be no goods to purchase. Economic contributions would have to be on a compulsory basis, and goods and services would have to be rationed out by the government in one way or another free of charge.

It is significant to note that in all countries of the world today the two systems are operating side by side. We have on the one hand a system under which goods are placed in the market at a price, signifying that the customer is free to select whatever he may desire or find use of, but that before he can remove any of his selection from the market he must redeem the price with credit. And it is generally understood that before he can have this credit he must himself contribute in some capacity to the goods marketed. On the other hand we have a system under which goods are free for all to enjoy without charge, but whose cost is billed to society as a whole.

The reason for maintaining the two systems is, of course, the fact that some goods by their very nature are such that they should be enjoyed in common in order to prevent the nuisance and cost of individual charging. If, for instance, highways should be subject to prices, toll gates would have to be erected at fixed intervals and travelers charged each time they passed a gate. If parks and playgrounds should be subject to prices, fences would have to be built around them to prevent anyone entering until he had paid a fee. Such a system would not only involve unnecessary expense, it would also create a less hospitable social environment.

On the other hand, if such goods as automobiles, jewelry, furniture, clothing, and the multitude of other items of individual choice and preference were to be distributed free of charge, we would no longer enjoy the freedom of choice. It would then fall on the government to ration out the goods produced in such a manner that each person would receive an equal share, to the extent that this was possible, the same house to live in, the same car to drive, the same clothes to wear. Furthermore, there would be little individual incentive to work or contribute economically, since the individual would receive no more of the fruits of labor whether he worked ambitiously or not; and economic contributions would have to be placed on a compulsory basis. We would have a system under which the government would be in sole paternal command, a system which is not likely to be tolerated in a freedom-loving country. It is unthinkable, therefore, that either of the two systems could operate without the other. Quite certainly we shall have one portion — the greater portion — of the national product placed in the market at a price, free for all to choose from, and the other portion — goods of a more social nature — commonly enjoyed and charged for.

3. Taxation

The presence of these two systems operating side by side within the economy creates some complex problems of financing or income divisioning which could be evaluated by different standards depending on our viewpoint of the circumstances involved. If we should consider the two systems as separate and independent of each other, we would have two basically different sectors within the economy, a private sector which produced marketed or priced goods and in which monetary income was paid, and a social sector which produced free goods and services and in which no monetary income was paid. Economic contributions in the private sector, then, would be on a voluntary basis, since the monetary reward would provide the necessary incentive. In the social sector contributions would have to be on a compulsory basis. This would necessitate an ordinance obligating each citizen to spend part of his working time in the social sector without monetary reward sufficient to produce the free goods and services. If the proportions of the two sectors should be eighty per cent and twenty per cent respectively, each citizen would be called upon to contribute twenty per cent of his working time in the social sector without monetary income.

Such an arrangement, however, could hardly be considered practical; and even if it were, it would involve an unnecessary shifting of the working force between the two sectors. It will seem more sensible that those in the private sector should remain in that sector, if they so wish, and that those in the social sector should remain there. But this means that each person in either sector should work twenty percent of his time without pay, or, if he receives income for his full time, he should work at eighty per cent of full pay. Those who remained in the social sector could not possibly be expected to work their full time without pay. They are producing not only their own share of the free goods and services but also the share enjoyed by those in the private sector and which should have been produced by them. The loss of money income incurred by the production of free goods and services must be shared equally between all concerned, implying that each person can expect to receive a rate of income which is lower than the price value of the goods he produces.

A difficulty arises from the unavoidable fact that the total monetary income in the course of production and distribution has a tendency to accrue to those in the private sector, that is, to producers, manufacturers and dealers who have the goods to sell. In the process of producing and selling goods they receive the full price of these goods, thereby collecting not only their own share of the national income but also the share belonging to those in the social sector. The social sector has no goods to sell and receives no income. This means that the overpaid part of the income accruing to the private sector must be deducted coincident with the paying of income to the social sector. This is what is known as taxation.

4. Comments on Taxation

In this connection we shall present three important generalizations concerning taxation. In the first place we shall conclude that *taxation is an act of deducting overpayment.* This statement may not appear correct to each and every person concerned who may feel that he is not overpaid; but what we mean is that the taxes levied on the private sector of the economy are not a charge for the free goods and services but rather a readjustment of monetary income. The total money income of the population as a whole cannot be more than the price value of the goods produced by the private sector; but since this sector in the course of producing and selling goods collects most or all of the monetary income while the sector producing free goods and services collects little or nothing, a readjustment must take place. The taxes levied on the private sector, therefore, is not a part of the income of this sector; rather it is income belonging to the social sector but which has accrued to the private sector by an error in distribution. Taxation corrects this error by deducting the overpayment commensurate with the income paid to the social sector.

From the same reasoning we must conclude, also, that in calculating the national income we cannot justifiably include in this income money taxed by the government in consideration of public finance. To do so would be to count this income twice. The true figure of national income must be arrived at by enumerating the income which actually belongs to the recipients of this income, not income which belongs to others and which must be deducted in the inevitable course of income readjustment.

Our second generalization is that *if each and every person received only the income that properly belonged to him, taxation would be unnecessary.* To a great many people this statement, again, will appear questionable. We have grown so accustomed to taxation that we would find it difficult to see how the government could operate without taxes. We would conclude that if the government did not levy direct taxes it would levy indirect taxes deducted from source or included in the price of the commodities we had to purchase. Suppose, however, that we should live under a system of complete socialism, a system under which all instruments of production and distribution belonged to the state and each and every one engaged in some economic activity was employed under one payroll — the government. Suppose, also, that we had known no other system. Under these circumstances we would not be conscious of any such thing as taxation, since taxation under such a system would be completely unnecessary. The government would already be in possession of the national income, and public finance would be a matter of distribution, not of levying taxes. Each group of people, whether engaged in building roads, erecting power lines, or manufacturing light bulbs, would, of course, receive its share of the payroll; and the total volume of income would be adjusted in accordance with the total price of the goods produced, or so as to balance production and distribution. If the total price of the goods marketed in any given production period should amount to $100,000,000 the total monetary income of the nation would also be placed at or near $100,000,000, irrespective of the fact that some people were engaged in price producing occupations, others in social services. Taxation under such a system would be justified only if by some blunder or miscalculation too much income had been distributed, and the error had to be corrected.

In the Soviet Union taxes have been imposed on the public despite socialism and despite the fact that most of the people are employed by the state. The reason is, of course, that the Soviet Government has been unable to control incomes. Monetary income has been distributed in such reckless abundance and in such disregard for the volume of prices or the volume of goods produced that the market has been depleted of goods and the surplus credit is a useless figure of promise on ink and paper. Of recent years, however, there has been a determined effort on the part of the Government to bring production into balance with distribution, and thereby, also, to abolish taxation. If the Soviet Government can accomplish this feat and establish an economy in which the market inventory remains balanced without rationing and without taxation, it could certainly boast of a much more orderly and a much more world respected social order than has hitherto been the case. It would, in fact, accomplish through socialism the aims and objects of Balanced Distribution which constitute the objective of the present plan.

This plan, however, does not advocate socialism, even if such a system should facilitate public finance. Undoubtedly it would be easier to clean chimneys if houses were built so that they could be turned upside down. So also it would be simpler to finance social services and undertakings if all people were made employees of the state. But what we must ask ourselves in each and every case is whether the move is worth the cost. In the opinion of the majority of the people in the Western world a move to replace private initiative with a system of universal wages would definitely be a step backwards. What we want is free enterprise, private ownership, individual initiative, the freedom to own and operate our own productive establishments, and the freedom to join in any business or economic pursuit that we might desire. But this means, also, that we may have to contend with the awkward system of overpayment and taxation.

There is a hope, however, that under a system of price and credit control taxation can be greatly simplified. Through co-operation between the different agencies of control, it seems possible that overpayment in many cases could be prevented, thus making personal taxes unnecessary. Overpayment and taxation have become such a tradition in our society that even government employees are overpaid and then taxed by their own employer. If overpayment can be avoided, it seems reasonable that this should be done. We might ask ourselves the question: why pay the one day more income to a person than rightly belongs to him and the next day apply force to withdraw the overpayment? It seems more sensible that if possible we should pay to each person the income which rightly belongs to him, and then make no attempt to take this income away from him.

5. Taxation as a Means of Credit Control

The third generalization in our series is that *taxation by the central government is a means of credit control exclusively*. This statement applies especially to a system of price and credit control, but it is true even today. The old concept that the purpose of taxation is to provide the government with spending money must be discarded. As already pointed out in the preceding chapter, the government could quite easily finance all its expenditures without taxation were it not for the fact that this would lead to credit inflation. There is absolutely nothing in the tax money, at least under a check system, that can be used again. This money, materially speaking, consists of a collection of useless papers which must be disposed of or destroyed. Neither the papers nor the numbers they convey can be used again. Financing is done by placing new numbers on new papers independent of those discarded.

This reasoning, however, does not mean to imply that taxation hereby is any the less important. Discontinuing taxation would be the surest way to disaster. The combined expenditures of the

Canadian and United States governments at present amount to in the neighborhood of one hundred billion dollars annually, which, if figured out in time, would amount to more than three thousand dollars per second. We can easily imagine what would happen if a $3,000 check was issued every second of the day and night throughout the years, each adding to the money volume already in circulation, without any credit being withdrawn through taxation. Under the present system it would lead to a galloping inflation of prices and the eventual collapse of the money system. Under central price control it would lead to credit inflation, depletion of the market inventory, hoarding of scarce commodities, and the final repudiation of the currency. Generally speaking, if one hundred billion dollars of new credit is added to the outstanding credit volume through government expenditures, one hundred billion, or near this amount, may also have to be deducted from this volume through taxation, in order to maintain the necessary credit control.

The fact remains, however, that we cannot use in our finances credit which has been levied in taxes, whether we should wish to do so or not. We may be able to use the same amount of credit, but we cannot use the same credit. The reason that people are called upon to remit their tax obligations to the federal treasury in the form of checks is that the government must satisfy itself that the overpaid credit accruing to people through the sale of goods has been deducted. If this could otherwise be ascertained, there would be no need to enforce any remittance of tax money or checks. Taxes, as a matter of fact, are paid the moment that people's deposit accounts are debited, or when their incomes are adjusted. Consider, for instance, the case that John Brown prepares to pay his tax of $200 to the federal government. In doing so he will, as a rule, proceed to draw a certified check on his bank account and send it to the federal treasury. The moment he draws this check at the bank, his bank account is reduced by $200, and the tax, therefore, is paid to the satisfaction of the federal government. It would now be completely unnecessary for John Brown to send his check to the treasury, provided that the government could otherwise be informed or convinced that $200 has been debited against John Brown's account. If John Brown immediately upon drawing this check at the bank should proceed to burn or destroy it, he would save the government the trouble of disposing of it. The reason for sending it to the federal treasury is that the government must satisfy itself that John Brown's account has been debited as requested.

The same is true in regard to the nation's taxpayers as a whole. Suppose that as a result of government spendings it should be found necessary to tax from the public one hundred billion dollars in the interest of credit control, and that the people should voluntarily proceed to draw these hundred billions from their bank accounts or savings and destroy all evidence of it, they would save the government a considerable amount of trouble and expense. Sending one hundred billion dollars in checks to the federal treasury would burden the government with an unproductive task of collecting and destroying all these checks. Yet we cannot see how it could otherwise be done. The government must remove excess credit from people's possession, if it is to carry on its program of spendings; and the only way to make sure that this is done is to compel remittance of taxes. There is no hope that the people would destroy their own credit.

6. Balancing of Distribution

Balanced distribution could be realized either by adjusting the volume of credit issued through government expenditure or the volume of credit withdrawn through taxation, although the latter process seems to be the more logical. Increasing the outstanding credit volume could be accomplished either by bringing government expenditures above taxation or by lowering taxation below expenditures. Reducing the outstanding credit volume, whenever such is found necessary, could be accomplished either by raising taxation above expenditures or by lowering expenditures below taxation.

It would be difficult to predict at any one time what financial balance will be necessary to maintain a balanced distribution, deficit financing, surplus financing, or a balanced budget. A balanced budget may be instrumental in maintaining a balanced distribution, but not necessarily so. There are other factors besides public finance, such as private bank lendings, savings and spendings, which have their bearing on distribution balance; and any such factor will help to determine what the government must do. The only true gauge by which to be guided in the matter of proper financing is the supply condition of the national market inventory. If more goods are withdrawn from the market than are deposited and shortages are threatened, the government is overfinancing and must either cut expenditures or increase taxation. If the opposite condition should be manifest, the government is underfinancing and must either boost expenditures or reduce taxation. The task of properly balancing distribution is unconditional. The object must be to maintain at all times an optimum market reserve.

The market inventory is the government's purse. When the market is well supplied with goods the government is in a healthy financial position and can afford to increase expenditures or reduce taxation. When the market inventory is at a critical stage and shortages are threatened, the financial position of the government is weak, and it may be necessary to cut expenditures or increase taxation. Budget figures or bank balance figures have nothing to do with public finance under Controlled Distribution. The financial strength of the government is indicated by the condition of the market, not by that of the bank. Whether or not the government can afford an expensive undertaking or can afford additional allocations and allowances will depend on the market supply of goods, the goods which constitute the source of government finance. A sure sign of national well-being is a well stocked market.

Judging from this criterion we could not help drawing our attention to the present economy with a feeling of discomfort. We have today a market teeming with goods of all descriptions and millions of willing hands waiting for an opportunity to supply more goods, but a population in want of the purchasing power with which to buy them; yet the government makes no attempt to increase credit. With a stupendous abundance of goods and services which under Balanced Distribution would constitute a huge blessing in the form of increased public purchasing power, the government is pursuing a program of crippling taxation which keeps the purchasing power constantly depressed and prevents us from coming into possession of the wealth that would otherwise be ours. And the reason is, of course, that the government could not do otherwise. It has no power at its disposal to increase purchasing power or to do anything to relieve the situation, and the best it can do under the circumstances is to maintain a fixed level of purchasing power deficiency. Any attempt to increase credit or purchasing power would simply raise prices with no benefit to the cause intended. It would be a frustrating experience of trying to increase the number of goods units with the population struggling to reduce the size of these units in proportion.

Those who blame the government for its failure to provide markets and jobs should need to reassess their judgement of the circumstances involved. Without price control no political party of whatever name or political leaning could ever solve the present problem, or even mitigate it, except as a temporary disturbance. With millions of people in charge of prices, each ready to heave prices with first easing of sales resistance, the only course open to the government is to maintain purchasing power deficiency and sales difficulty sufficient to keep prices within reasonable limits; and no other government could do any better. Any suggestion of improvement from any political source which did not include price control would have little chance of ever doing any good.

From the standpoint of Balanced Distribution the present situation is not desperate; on the contrary it is extremely fortunate. It bears evidence of teeming riches in goods and services, which can be released through price and credit control, riches which now are tied from our reach by the hopeless escalator condition of run-away prices. As soon as prices are anchored by the implementation of price control, and public financing proceeds from the strength of the market reserve, this abundance can come to our avail. The government will immediately be blessed by a huge reservoir of now latent financial resources, which can come to the benefit of the public in the form of reduced taxation or otherwise. Thus, the overproduction, or market glut, which now appears to be our misfortune, will turn into a blessing, and will greatly assist in any financial undertaking which the government finds advantageous to pursue.

7. The Necessity of Preventing Overdistribution

It has been suggested that when unemployment exists the government should launch an extensive program of public works, build roads and bridges, hospitals and schools, develop parks, launch housing projects, and should meet the expense of this program through deficit financing. If such a program was preceded by price control, it would be highly commendable, since it would, perhaps, produce reemployment at a faster rate than through the ordinary channels of industry, and the new credit so created would find its way to the market in the form of increased demand and would further boost employment and production. Without price control the program would produce very few beneficial effects. It would increase purchasing power for a limited period until prices had risen sufficiently to neutralize the increase; and by this time it would be necessary to resort to further deficit financing and further public works, with the inevitable result of further price increases; and the net result would be a more rapidly increasing price level with some increase in employment and economic activity. There is still a great deal of wishful thinking on the part of some people that price inflation will not take place as long as unemployment exists, despite all empirical evidence in support of it. If we are to boost purchasing power and realize full employment and full capacity production, our first step must be to anchor prices. The second step in the program of supplementing the purchasing power, the issue of a sufficient volume of credit, will not involve any problem, nor will it be necessary to build roads and bridges in order to carry it out. Clearly, the simplest, and most effortless task is to increase the outstanding credit volume, whether this is accomplished by means of issuing more (through public expenditures) or withdrawing less (through taxation). The credit volume, numerically speaking, is already more than sufficient to hold the price level; and if prices were anchored, there would soon be enough purchasing power to balance distribution without any special efforts by the government.

The fact is that under Price and Credit Control the problem facing the credit control commission (or government) will not be how to create enough purchasing power but, on the contrary, to prevent this purchasing power from becoming overabundant and causing scarcity of marketed goods. The promise of markets and increased demand will inevitably cause a greater demand for bank loans to finance new enterprises and increased output. Capitalization and increased inventory accumulation might cause a suspicion that goods will be in short supply and that the time has come to increase purchases. Money circulation will increase, and credit will expand. All logical calculations point to the possibility of purchasing power expansion from private sources; but even though the government should be called upon temporarily to issue more credit than it withdraws, or, vice versa, to withdraw less credit than it issues, it is clear that the prime duty of the government will be to prevent overdistribution and scarcity. Contrary to the conditions existing at present, overdistribution and scarcity will be a far greater hazard than underdistribution and surpluses, and the temptation by the government to overissue will be greater than that to underissue, considering that it is more pleasant to distribute money to the public than to take this money away from them. Taxation, however, is an inescapable duty, whether pleasant or not, for upon it depends the balancing of distribution. Failure to tax and withdraw enough credit from people's possession would cause scarcity, panic buying, hoarding, and all the evil of overdistribution.

It will be understood that the sole purpose of taxation under Controlled Distribution is to prevent credit inflation and scarcity. All expenditures of the federal government proceed from new credit, independent of any credit withdrawn through taxation. Most or all credit is issued by means of checks and withdrawn by means of checks; but even if notes and coins are used, the credit they carry is issued and withdrawn, not circulated, since currency held by the federal government does not embody credit. The credit instruments, or carriers, may continue to exist, but the credit they carry is issued anew with government expenditures and ceases to exist with taxation. Taxation is not necessary to finance expenditures; it is necessary to prevent scarcity of marketed goods.

With regard to this fiscal action, it will seem appropriate to divide the government into two executive branches, the Allocation Branch and the Control Branch, each with its specific function. The Allocation Branch finances all government expenditures with new credit on the basis of need alone. It allocates money for all government undertakings, pays all wages and salaries, distributes pensions and allowances, grants loans. It spends money on all projects which are considered necessary or desirable, health, education, public works. Despite the fact that it finances more or less independent of "revenue," it must economize and avoid expenditures not consistent with efficiency or necessity, since any such expenditures would lower over-all productivity.

The Control Branch has one purpose, and one alone: to tax and withdraw (destroy) credit sufficient to balance distribution. It operates independent of what the government spends. A balanced budget is incidental. It must base its taxation policy on market conditions alone. It must conduct a continued study of total supply and total demand and govern itself accordingly. If at any time the total demand for goods and services should be in excess of supply and shortages should threaten, it must immediately take steps to increase taxation and reduce public purchasing power. If demand should be insufficient to absorb the products of industry, and inventories should have a tendency to accumulate, it must reduce taxation and boost purchasing power. Its taxation policy has nothing to do with public expenditures, bank balances, or budget figures. It has one vital duty to perform, a duty upon which the welfare of the whole economy rests, the balancing of distribution.

CHAPTER IX

CONFLICTING SOCIAL OBJECTIVES

1. Contrasting Impacts of Savings

According to our income-price equation the national monetary income must be equal to the price value of the goods to be distributed plus savings. This means that any addition to the credit savings held by the public will automatically boost incomes to the same measured extent. And the reason for this is obvious. When people save, they leave in the market goods which they would otherwise withdraw, and in order to balance distribution as before the government will have to issue or leave with the public an additional volume of credit equal to the savings, so that this savings demand is met without affecting distribution. If, for instance, during a given period the people of the nation should pile up an addition to their credit savings amounting to one billion dollars, they would, other things being equal, leave in the market a billion dollars' worth of goods which they would otherwise have withdrawn. Consequently the fiscal authority in control of distribution could permit an extra billion dollars of credit to remain with the public in the form of reduced fiscal levies without the fear of an unbalanced distribution. It is to be understood, of course, that if during a second period the people should reverse their action and dissave to the amount of one billion dollars, they would, *ceteris paribus,* withdraw from the market a billion dollars in goods above their usual purchases, and the government would also have to reverse its action and withdraw by means of taxation or otherwise one billion dollars of credit over and above the ordinary levies to prevent shortages. This means, in other words, that any fluctuation in the demand for savings will be met by a corresponding fluctuation in the outstanding credit volume through government fiscal action. Savings will tend to increase incomes while spendings or dissavings will tend to reduce incomes.

It is significant to note that under the present system the very opposite seems to be true. Savings appear to reduce incomes while dissavings appear to increase incomes. In fact, some economists have suggested that if the total income during a given period should be $100,000,000 but that $5,000,000 of this income was saved, the income during a second period could not be more than $95,000,000. This viewpoint testifies to the inflexibility of the present money system. It implies that the money volume is a fixed quantity which can neither be increased nor decreased and that if someone saves or hoards part of this money he is helping to strangle the economy by keeping money out of circulation. Incomes and spendings according to this theory must correspond. No one can have income unless someone spends the money. The money must somehow come from the other person, the other firm, the other company, or the other country. The only way to increase incomes according to this theory is to increase spendings. Concomitant with this conception, also, the saver or "hoarder" is condemned as the scapegoat who contributes to the tragedy of economic stagnation and unemployment.

Looked upon from the standpoint of a Balanced Distribution, this theory becomes absurd. It will be clear to anyone that the credit we receive in return for our productive contributions is not the real income. The real income is the actual goods and services which we select in exchange for this credit. Credit is simply the papers or the markings on paper which entitle us to claim our real income in kind from the general market; and if we fail to claim these goods, we have received nothing in return for our work or our economic contributions. If, for instance, a person should contribute to the general market reserve a million dollars' worth of goods — supposing this to be possible — and should receive in return a million dollars in monetary credit which he would save or "hoard" for the remainder of his lifetime, he would actually have presented the nation with a free gift of one million dollars. The million dollars' worth of goods which actually belonged to him would contribute to swell the market reserve; and in order to maintain production-consumption balance as before, the government could permit an extra million dollars to remain with the public in the form of reduced taxation. Thus the "hoarder" would automatically benefit the nation to the value of one million dollars in income at the expense of his own.

There is also another striking example of contrast between contemporary economic thought on the subject of savings and the circumstances obtaining under a system of price and credit control. Thus, for instance, it is generally held that if a person converts his savings into government bonds, he will render assistance to public finance; if he keeps his savings in a bank, he will render less assistance, or none at all; but if he saves by keeping currency in his own home, he will do harm by keeping money out of circulation. This implies, in other words, that if a person orients his savings so that others can use his money, he will assist the nation's economy; but if he saves so that no one else can use his savings, he will help to deteriorate the conditions by holding on to money which others — including the government — must use in their financing.

This viewpoint again becomes absurd when looked upon from the standpoint of a Balanced Distribution. A person who saves, let us say one thousand dollars, will benefit public finance because he leaves one thousand units of goods in the market, not because he leaves the record of this saving with the government or with the bank or with any other agency. His real saving consists of a thousand goods units left in the national market reserve, the reserve which constitutes the government's source of finance; and by means of this saving he has strengthened the financial position of the government to the same extent. It does not matter where he keeps the papers which record the particulars of this savings, whether he keeps them in a government office, in a bank, or under the mattress in his own home. The possession of these papers by the government could not possibly be of any value, except in so far as it would tie up credit and prevent the creditor from spending it; but the benefit would be the same if the papers were kept in any other place.

2. Contrasting Impacts of Spendings

But whereas savings under the present system appear to be detrimental to the economy, spendings, appear to be advantageous, a situation which again presents a direct conflict between the two systems. If under Controlled Distribution the consuming public should embark on an unusual spending spree, shortages of marketed goods would likely appear, and the government would be compelled to impose additional taxation or other countermeasures sufficiently punitive to cope with the situation, measures which obviously would constitute a loss of income. Today economists and politicians as well as the huge masses of salesmen are joined in solid bloc to urge spendings on the hypothesis that this campaign is the road to prosperity, that spendings will set the limit of our national income and that, therefore, any increase in spendings will help to solve the problem of marketing and unemployment.

The strange fact, however, is that the nation would stand aghast at the suggestion that the government should inflate the credit volume, even though this would be the simplest way to increase spendings. The idea is that such a move would cause price inflation and depreciation of the currency, whereas the spending of money already in circulation will not affect prices. The theory, of course, is false. The fact is that price movements are caused by fluctuations in spendings, not necessarily by fluctuations in the credit volume. The reason that price inflation is most likely to follow an inflation of credit is that the additional credit as a matter of course will manifest itself in increased spendings. But increased spendings generated by a more rapid circulation of the money already in existence would cause the self-same thing.

The only difference between the two methods of promoting spendings is that the one is more successful than the other. Advertising and sales pressure has become so commonplace and standardized that any additional pressure to spend or invest will have little effect on overall spendings. This sales pressure may be instrumental in maintaining a greater velocity of circulation than would otherwise be the case, but any spectacular increase in spendings generated from this source is unlikely, and the practice, fortunately, is entirely safe. If this pressure on the consuming public should be successful in increasing spendings, it would cause price inflation just as certain as an inflation of credit.

3. Contrasting Impacts of Supply

Under a system of price and credit control the government is financing from the strength of the national market reserve, and the more goods that can be pushed into this reserve, the more the income and the more the nation will prosper. It is with respect to this situation that we again find a direct conflict between the two systems. The present economy appears to prosper with scarcity and suffer want with abundance. If by some supernatural cause a large portion of the national market reserve should dissipate, the nation would undoubtedly be blessed by a period of prosperity. Retailers with reduced supply of goods on hand would increase their orders from wholesalers. Wholesalers with reduced supplies and increased orders would doubly increase their orders from manufacturers and producers. Manufacturers and producers, who also had reduced supplies with greatly increased orders, would employ more labor and boost production. There would be a rush for bank loans to start new enterprises, and the credit volume would expand. Prices and profits would rise, and industry would flourish. The population would have more purchasing power, temporarily at least, and consumer demand would increase. Retailers, experiencing increased demand and rising prices, would again increase their orders, ad inf. The whole economy would be booming.

If on the other hand the market inventory should miraculously increase, leaving more goods in the hands of producers, manufacturers and dealers, the nation would likely be in for a period of depression. Retailers and wholesalers would reduce their orders for merchandise. Producers and manufacturers would curtail production and lay off workers. Banks would recall loans, and credit volume would contract. Prices and profits would drop, and consumer demand would dwindle.

It seems evident that if the same miracles should occur under Controlled Distribution where credit must be adjusted to requirement by compensatory public finance, the very opposite conditions would obtain. A substantial loss of marketed goods would inevitably result in a corresponding loss of public purchasing power or income, and this loss would affect the public as a whole. The government would have to suppress consumer demand to meet the emergency, and a likely method of doing so would be to impose extra heavy taxation for an appropriate period until the market reserve had again been built up to its optimum level. On the other hand, an opposite miracle by which the market inventory received a substantial addition would inevitably come as a welcome present. The authority in control of distribution would have to supply the population with a substantial addition of credit through the medium of deficit financing to absorb the increased supply, and the public in general would benefit, either in increased wealth or increased leisure, whichever they would choose.

The explanation of this phenomenal contrast between the two systems is that today we have an unbalanced or low-purchasing-power economy. We have a superabundance of supply in the form of unusable specialities but an inadequacy of purchasing power with which we should gain interchanged access to these goods; and if we receive a further addition to our supply, the economy becomes even more unbalanced, and the conditions worsen. If, on the other hand, a substantial portion of our supply is removed, supply and demand moves nearer to the level of balance, and conditions improve.

Naturally the proper method of establishing balance between supply and demand is to increase demand, not to reduce supply; but this we cannot do. Without price control we have no means at our disposal to increase purchasing power or demand, except for a very limited period. Our next attempt, therefore, in the struggle to effect supply-demand equilibrium, is to reduce supply, to take goods off the market in one way or another, or to prevent them from entering. But even this method is futile, for no sooner have marketing conditions by this action eased than prices begin rising to reduce purchasing power commensurate with the reduction in supply. We cannot escape the Law of Sales Resistance as long as the same unbridled price competition prevails. Reducing supply will simply reduce purchasing power to the same extent, but the purchasing power will always be insufficient as before.

It is significant to note, however, that efforts to reduce marketed or marketable goods have frequently been resorted to during many decades past in an attempt to attain balance between supply and demand. Governments, in fact, have sometimes engaged in the most effective of these supply-reducing methods, viz., the direct destruction of goods, the burning of thousands of tons of coffee, the destroying of mountains of potatoes, and the dumping of pigs into the sea. A more common method, however, is to stock away goods in government warehouses, where they are removed from direct contact with the market. The American Commodity Credit Corporation, for example, has for many years past continued to stock up surplus farm products in magazines and warehouses throughout the land. The stocks at this date have reached a value of over twelve billion dollars. It costs the taxpayers of the United States a billion dollars a year just to store the goods and keep them from rotting. And these are goods which can never be used or marketed as long as the present pricing system prevails. Economically and politically they constitute a burden, and the only reason for not destroying them is the necessity of preventing public resentment. Yet the government has no other alternative than to stock up more goods, another magazine, another warehouse, to keep the farmers occupied. These farmers have nowhere else to go — all other lines of production are "overproduced" — and to flood the market with these goods would add perhaps a million farmers to the unemployed ranks. It is a problem which cannot be solved until such a time as we can create and control purchasing power. The purchasing power of the nation is now inexorably insufficient to absorb the goods produced at full capacity; and even though keeping goods away from the market will not solve the problem, it appears to be the right thing to do. The very opposite government action of flooding the market with goods would undoubtedly be more beneficial in the long run, since this would lower prices and restore the purchasing power—by a painful process—to a point at which it would be no more insufficient than before, despite the increased volume of goods. But this action would appear unwarranted considering that it is goods (actually prices) that are abundant relative to purchasing power. Besides, it would in all certainty be met with violent opposition and protests, especially from farmers or those most adversely affected. Hence the government finds itself pressed to continue the hopeless struggle to stock away goods.

A controlled and balanced system of distribution will inevitably change the thinking on these matters, and radically so. No longer will it be thought advantageous to reduce or remove marketed goods. Granting that price and credit control is in competent hands and the rules of distribution control are fully complied with, supply and demand should always balance, irrespective of the volume of output; and, naturally, the more goods that can be brought into the national market under this condition, the more we will prosper. Every addition to the goods marketed will reflect in a corresponding addition to the national income. A tendency toward overproduction in any one line will be a welcome sign, since this will make possible the release of manpower or productive capacity from this line for other lines of production. A tendency toward overproduction in all lines would be an even greater testimony of economic welfare, since this would indicate a healthy financial position on the part of the government and precipitate an imminent increase in public income, either through increased government spendings or reduced taxation. The supreme national efforts, obviously, will be to maximize production and marketing, to promote maximum efficiency in production and distribution, to bring automation to its ultimate perfection, to remove overt as well as disguised unemployment or any wastage of labor or productive capacity, and make possible a greater affluence and more leisure.

4. Futile National Endeavors

The national efforts now pursued in a bid to relieve the problem of distribution and unemployment may appear logical when looked upon from the standpoint of prevailing circumstances. However, if looked upon from the standpoint of a future, more scientifically planned economy, many of these efforts would not make sense. Let us consider again some of these puzzling endeavors. Why, for instance, do we prescribe production quotas to limit output? Why do we pay farmers for not producing or for plowing under their crop? Why do we endeavor to export more than we import to establish a "favorable" trade balance? Why do we erect "protective" tariff walls to prevent goods from entering our country? Why do we destroy goods or store them away with no plan for their recovery? Why do we sometimes campaign against automation on the hypothesis that it takes away jobs? Why do we retain men in employment long after their services have been replaced by mechanization or do work by hand labor which could be done by machinery? Why do we endeavor to "create work", taking little thought of what this work will accomplish?

The argument is, as we know, that we do not have enough "work", but that we have too many goods; and one suggestion of relieving the situation is that we must export goods, especially goods which contain a considerable amount of labor. At the same time we must endeavor to bring in money from abroad, since this, according to the same fairy tale of the future, will "bring wealth into the country." We will readily admit a person to our country if he can show us a bundle of monetary credit and came to retire, but we will hesitate if he came to work and contribute to our national product. We will permit a citizen to ship all the goods he can across the border to some other country, but we will hesitate to permit him to purchase goods abroad. We will spend millions on tourist advertisements, because tourists will take away many of our goods and leave the papers of credit. We are worried lest our military personnel should be disbanded and added to our labor force, since this might cause a depression. We are contemplating plans to export workers, or to stop immigration, except for those who do not come to demand work. We are demanding reduced working hours as a means of creating more jobs. We are attempting to enact laws forbidding married women and older men to work or anyone to hold more than one job.

We are anxious that our prisoners should be occupied in hard labor, but we take care that they do not produce goods and compete with those already in the market. In a hundred and one ways we are endeavoring to prevent goods from being produced or from being added to our market inventory. We are waging a war against goods and services, the very goods and services which must bring us prosperity and economic supremacy in a divided world. We are throwing away our only effective weapons against communism. If our aim were to sabotage our nation in the interest of a communist victory, we could not do better.

This type of endeavor, even at best, is a costly wastage of time and effort, a hopeless struggle which could never bring the aims and objects aforeseen. In order to have a prosperous economy we must have a purchasing power level which attracts maximun output, a level of demand which encourages a continued expansion of production and marketing. Today we have a purchasing power level which remains constantly below physical capacity, thus acting to discourage output and economic growth; and as long as this condition prevails, no other action to improve conditions will do much good. An attempt to make the purchasing power sufficient by suppressing goods and services could never produce anything but a negative result.

There is no inconsistency or lack of integrity on the part of the government in dealing with the present problem. Any elected government in this hemisphere is undoubtedly acting in good faith. It is conscious of the communist threat and would do anything in its power to further the interest of the nation in a bid to dispel fear for the safety of free enterprise. The unfortunate circumstance is that the government under the present system has no authority to take corrective action. The control of purchasing power and distribution is in the hands of those who control prices, for they are the ones who "place the goods in the baskets." The government, through its action in issuing credit, is simply "supplying the empty baskets." It would be the simplest thing for the government to increase the numerical volume of credit even a hundredfold or a thousandfold or a millionfold, but the value of the credit unit would drop to a hundredth and to a thousandth and to a millionth of its previous value, and the purchasing power of the nation would be no greater than before. This, then, is the situation such as we see it today. We have a government which is expected to assume the responsibility for the welfare of the nation's economy, but which is deprived of the authority to create and control purchasing power, the lifeblood on which the welfare of the economy depends. The result is that this government, anxious to provide prosperity and full employment, finds itself compelled to take actions which logically conflict with national interest, to suppress goods and services, even though this is a sadly abortive substitute for a cure.

Those who blame the government for its inaction in solving the problem of distribution and unemployment yet who insist on unrestrained freedom to set prices do not use a logical line of reasoning. The government could solve the problem of distribution by the simplest of all actions, namely, to reduce taxes or interest rates, provided that this action was not frustrated by those who control the value of the credit. Our present economic troubles are not caused by any neglect to supply an adequate volume of money, numerically speaking, but by the failure to maintain the purchasing value of this money, a task for which the pricing public now are responsible. To remove one government from office and elect another to work under the same circumstances would serve no useful purpose.

5. Conclusion

The most tragic effect of the problem of distribution is not that it denies us a fairly high standard of living. The fact is that despite the loss of productivity suffered by the problem we are reasonably comfortable. Even the unemployed are being cared for, and many of them are quite satisfied with the arrangement. The sad part of the situation is that it places our economy in a weak defensive position on today's economic battlefield. It needlessly creates a humiliating sentiment among our people in the face of communism. It causes insecurity, fear, frustration, and anger. It creates and upholds communism and exposes free enterprise to the jeopardy of communist expansionism. It has encouraged communists to prognosticate our downfall and the inevitable triumph of communism, and it has enervated us to meet this challenge with bitterness and military protectionism, which could lead to utter disaster. It has inflated our mental image of communism to Gargantuan proportions and has made necessary a stupendous defense budget. The solution of the problem of distribution will deflate the phantom of communism and remove the need for military defense. It is our action in the near future that will determine the course of human events for centuries to come. It could lead to a world of free enterprise or a world of communism; but it could do more than that: it could lead to a life of prosperity, freedom and happiness, or a grotesque survival under a cloud of atomic fallout.

Our most urgent need at this time is a clear, unprejudiced view of the situation and of the course of action which will best serve our individual and national interests. What we need is men with vision and resourcefulness, especially young men who must make this world their future abode and their place of happiness. Our object should be to defeat communism, but to do this by economic means, not by military means; by construction, not by destruction. We must bring victory over communism, not by bitterness and hatred, not by senseless destruction of human life and property, not by wanton abandonment of decency and respect for those who want to live, but by sound, unbiased reasoning and planning for the betterment of our society; by removing unemployment and other causes of discontent and building a healthier, more prosperous and more agreeable economic and social life. This we can do, and the time to do it is now.

The inevitable conclusion is that we must place the control of purchasing power (prices and credit) in the hands of a responsible government. This is imperative, if our free-enterprise economy is to survive and prosper. It does not mean that we should assume a preference for government controls. On the contrary, the object should be to limit government controls to a minimum, in fact, to remove, if possible, many government controls now in effect. But what we must do is to institute government control of purchasing power, and to establish a permanently balanced system of distribution. This can be done, it must be done, and it will be done. It is a reform which can be delayed but which cannot be stopped, and there is no reason why it should not be done forthwith.

INDEX